Sensory Integration Strategies for Parents
SI at Home and School

By: Jeanne Sangirardi Ganz, OTR/L, BCP

First Edition

Biographical Publishing Company
Prospect, Connecticut

Sensory Integration Strategies
for Parents
SI at Home and School

First Edition

Published by:

Biographical Publishing Company
35 Clark Hill Road
Prospect, CT 06712-1011

Phone: 203-758-3661   Fax: 253-793-2618
e-mail: biopub@aol.com

PRINTED IN THE UNITED STATES OF AMERICA

Publisher's Cataloging-in-Publication Data

Ganz, Jeanne Sangirardi
Sensory Integration Strategies for Parents : SI at Home and School / by Jeanne Sangirardi Ganz.-- 1st ed.
    p. cm.
    ISBN 1-929882-51-3
    13 Digit ISBN 9781929882519
    1. Ganz, Jeanne Sangirardi   2. Sensory Integration Strategies.
    3. Sensory Integration Dysfunctions. 4. Child rearing and home care. 5. Special needs/special education.
    I. Title.
    Dewey Decimal Classification: 649
    Library of Congress Control Number: 2008924301

TABLE OF CONTENTS

Acknowledgements

The author would like to extend a very big thank you to Heather Ganz for her dedication and time, as well as her computer skills, that helped to make this book possible.

Thanks are also in order to Margaret Spring, JoAnne Walker, Karen Dwyer, and Lorraine Hemon.

INTRODUCTION

What can I do to help my child who has Sensory Integration Dysfunction? This is the foremost question on every parent's mind who faces life with a child with sensory integration dysfunction, or DSI, as it has come to be identified. This book is written to answer that very question. It is a book of ideas, strategies, and hints to help your child be successful despite the challenges of DSI. The book presents a brief overview of sensory integration dysfunction and its varied presentations. It then proceeds to offer strategies that may be helpful to accomplish everyday tasks. How do we help him to tolerate a haircut? How can I help her to print better? How can we help him to do his homework without falling apart? How can I get her to be calmer? How can we make school a better experience for our child? These and other questions will be addressed in a problem solving format. *Not all of the suggestions will be appropriate for every child and for every family. These suggestions are ideas and strategies that have been helpful for many children, but as a parent, you must decide which are most appropriate for* **your** *child and your family.*

So come along on a journey- a journey of exploration and learning, a journey of understanding, a journey of success.

IN THE MEANTIME...

Hopefully, you are reading this book because your child has already been identified as having sensory integration dysfunction and hopefully receiving treatment for it. This book provides strategies for helping your child get through the daily life events that are sometimes so challenging for children with sensory integration dysfunction. This is an "in the meantime" book that provides strategies to use until your child does not need them anymore. This book presents strategies to make some of the life tasks that are typically challenging for children with sensory integration dysfunction become easier. It combines sensory integration theory with behavioral support to decrease the trauma associated with these events. With sensory integration treatment, many of these activities will naturally become easier for your child. But *in the meantime,* haircuts and baths need to occur; parties, school, and social events must be attended; and, as they say, life goes on.

How should I use this book?

Use this book under the guidance of your occupational therapist who is treating your child for sensory integration dysfunction. If you do not have a therapist, or if you are looking for an evaluation, please see the recommendations at the close of this section. The suggestions are "food for thought" that may help you create a more pleasant and less stressful method of accomplishing these daily tasks with your child. Not every suggestion will be helpful or appropriate for your child or family. The goal of these suggestions is to offer alternative ways of looking at the situations your child faces, and to minimize any stressors that make the activity difficult to accomplish. The goal is to use as *few* of these strategies as needed to "get the job done" and to *decrease* the amount of strategies needed as your child progresses. The most success is seen when these strategies are no longer needed.

Another important intention of this book is to help your child look at and experience these tasks in a new way. This is to do what is called "reframe" the event. If we can help our children *learn* to experience an event in a pleasant way, they will expect those events to be pleasant in the future. For example, if every time a child brushes his teeth, he experiences an awful tasting toothpaste, he learns to fear or avoid brushing his teeth. However, if you change the taste to something delicious, he will now look forward to it. On a more complex level, if your child experiences pain and discomfort when her hair is brushed, we need to help change that experience through sensory and behavioral strategies to make her feel comfortable and secure. From another perspective, if your child *expects* to perform poorly in motor tasks, than those motor tasks are often avoided by your child. Consequently, your child may never become successful at those avoided tasks. If you provide just the right amount of support, you can help your child achieve the challenging tasks. This increases the chances that your child will not only repeat them, but continue to face the challenges and truly gain in skill and confidence.

We all learn to "expect" based on our experiences. Sometimes, even when the sensory challenges are diminished, children will hold on to their negative expectations and we see behavioral challenges. For example, if a child has learned that wearing blue jeans is uncomfortable, he may develop a "behavioral idea" that blue jeans are bad, or blue jeans are scary, or simply feel that "I do not wear blue jeans." They may react emotionally to requests to wear blue jeans because they have the *idea* that is hard to change. They sometimes hold onto that idea, even when they try on the blue jeans and see that they are no longer uncomfortable or that a new, different brand is a comfortable style. These strategies should help to gradually "reframe" those *ideas* and make the task a tolerable one. This takes time, patience, and a very positive attitude from those adults who are helping children with this process. When parents feel sure and confident that their child can succeed, they help to empower their child to do just that.

How can I find a therapist to work with my child?

There are several avenues for finding a therapist who is knowledgeable about sensory processing. You may want to ask other parents, teachers, or your pediatrician for personal referrals. You can also contact the American Occupational Therapy Association (AOTA), your local OT association, a local university that has an OT program, or the pediatric department of your local hospital. You can visit the Sensory Integration International, SI Network, Western Psychological Services, or special interest support group websites for therapist locators. School districts may also have information for children aged three and up. If your child is under three years of age he/she may qualify to receive services through your county's Early Intervention Program.

EDUCATE, COMMUNICATE, PARTICIPATE

An Overview

An effective way to view sensory processing management strategies is that it is a threefold process. The first step is to **educate,** the second to **communicate**, and lastly to **participate.** These are described below.

STEP ONE: EDUCATE

First, educate yourself about sensory processing in general. You can do this by reading books, attending lectures, checking websites, speaking to professionals, and speaking to other parents. A list of resources is included in this book, under the Education section, but new information is always becoming available.

Secondly, educate yourself about your child. Each child is unique and presents a pattern of sensory processing that is individual. It may take some time to do this as there is, as of yet, no crystal ball into the brain. Even medical testing, therapeutic testing, and educational testing are not absolute. It takes time and patience. Be open to seeing that your child may function differently in different settings and with different people. Your child may be very different in school than at home. Communicating with others in the different settings will help you learn more about your child.

STEP TWO: COMMUNICATE

Communicate with your child and with others. Communication is essential in all areas. You will need to become very good at communicating with your child as well as with the people who interact with your child.

How do you communicate with your child? How do you speak with your child? This will vary by your child's developmental level as well as language development. Many children with sensory modulation dysfunction also have communication difficulties. You may need to simplify concepts, use pictures, or even storybooks to help the communication process.

Communication with others is also essential. You will likely find yourself explaining and teaching others about sensory integration. You can use books, handouts, and web sites to share with others. You will most likely need to explain to family members, friends, and sometimes to teachers and other professionals.

As parents, you often see aspects of your child that others do not. Communicate what you see to professionals who are working with your child. By the same token, professionals may often see aspects of your child that you do not get to see as well, especially at school. Communication is very important in order to fully understand your child's needs, and how those needs might vary in different settings.

STEP THREE: PARTICIPATE

Participation, as used here, refers to two things.

First, it is the act of engaging in activities that provide sensory "nutrition" for your child. These are games, toys, and activities that help promote the processing of sensory information to improve sensory modulation and sensory integration. Some examples of these activities, as well as a list of resources for these types of sensory integration activities, are included in this book. They may be found in the "Participate" section.

Second, participation refers to providing the activities or procedures, which make engaging in life events, pleasant and natural for your child. How can you help your child to participate and enjoy all that life has to offer? This is a major focus of this book.

Sensory Integration Strategies for Parents

EDUCATE

Step One

This section includes an overview of sensory integration, sensory modulation, and the various presentations of sensory integration dysfunction.

It also includes an environment analysis with general concepts regarding the sensory aspects of environments.

In the final pages of this section you will find the *Parent Resources*, which lists books, publications, websites, and catalog company information for your reference.

SENSORY INTEGRATION OVERVIEW

The theory and treatment of sensory integration was developed by Dr. A. Jean Ayres, OTR in the 1960's in an attempt to understand and explain some of the connections between learning and the functioning of the nervous system. She developed specific testing and treatment to provide what she felt was the optimal treatment for learning disabled children who had sensory processing problems. Not all children with learning disabilities have sensory integrative dysfunction but sensory integrative dysfunction often has an impact on learning and behavior.

Sensory integration is a normal process by which the sensory systems provide information about our bodies and the world around us. The brain and the rest of the nervous system takes that information and organizes it so that we can learn, move, and behave normally. This is sensory processing, or sensory integration. All people process sensory information, some more efficiently than others.

What are the sensory systems important to sensory integration?

The **tactile system** is the sense of touch. It tells us that we are being touched, what is touching us, about pressure on the skin, temperature, and pain. It helps to develop motor skills, attention span, and an awareness of our bodies. It helps us feel comfortable and secure in the world and around other people.

There are two gravity senses that tell us about

movement. They are the vestibular and proprioceptive systems.

The **vestibular system** is the gravity sense. It tells us if we are moving or not, and how fast we are moving. It also tells us in which direction we are moving and helps us feel comfortable and safe as we move. The vestibular system enables us to develop good eye muscle control, visual perception, and attention span. It helps us coordinate the two sides of the body and develop a hand dominance. It effects our muscle tone, or the ability of our muscles to get ready to move, and helps us to balance. The vestibular system has an influence on almost every part of the brain. It is a very powerful sensory system that helps us organize our bodies and ourselves. It even has connections in the brain to centers that control our emotions and feelings.

The **proprioceptive system** provides information about our bodies. It tells us what position our bodies are in and where our body is in the environment. The sensations arise from joints and muscles and from their activity. Proprioception helps us learn to use skilled movement. It helps us feel comfortable as we move through the environment.

The senses that are more commonly known are the visual system (vision), the olfactory system (smell), the auditory system (hearing), and the gustatory system (taste). These sensory systems all work with the primary systems, described above, to provide additional information about our external environment. They add to the information we receive from the tactile, vestibular, and proprioceptive systems.

When the normal process of sensory integration is not efficient we label it sensory integration dysfunction. This simply means that parts of this processing system are not providing information reliably. Sensory integration dysfunction (labeled DSI) can interfere with an individual's ability to attend, develop motor skills, regulate behavior and organize tasks, complete self care skills (for example, dressing and eating), develop visual and auditory skills, and to feel comfortable in the environment.

SENSORY INTEGRATION DYSFUNCTION

Sensory integrative dysfunction (DSI) is a disorder of the organization and processing of sensory information. It is due to an irregularity or disorder in brain function. Many people with sensory integrative dysfunction have difficulties in learning and behavior. This impacts on several areas of daily life. Not all people with sensory integrative dysfunction have all of the problems described below, but many have several problem areas.

Poor sensory integration can interfere with **motor skills**. When the information received from the tactile and proprioceptive systems is not processed efficiently an individual will likely have a problem in **praxis or motor planning**. Praxis is the ability to figure out how to use one's body and tools in a skilled manner. Whenever we learn a new motor skill or change an already learned one we need to use praxis (motor planning). Remember the first time you learned to tie your shoe, write in script, or ride a bike? You needed praxis. An individual with poor praxis will not only have a great deal of difficulty learning tasks such as these, but will also find it difficult to learn to use different size lines on the paper, to tie a new pair of shoes with different laces, or to ride a friend's bike. People with dyspraxia (or poor motor planning) may move more slowly or have trouble following directions. They may need to control the environment to avoid the stress or embarrassment of failure to perform as others do. These individuals may have difficulty with dressing skills and look clumsy. Many people with dyspraxia need to spend a great deal of energy to accomplish motor tasks, which takes away from their ability to concentrate on cognitive or academic tasks.

Some individuals with sensory integration dysfunction have a deficit in **bilateral coordination** due to poor **vestibular/proprioceptive** processing. This interferes with the ability to use both sides of the body together such as in jumping jacks, lacing and sewing, or even holding paper down to write. They may be delayed in, or fail to develop or use, a dominant hand. They may struggle to sequence, or put themselves or their environment in order. Some individuals have difficulty orienting themselves around the midline of the body and may actually miss the middle of words or sentences when reading. These individuals may also look clumsy and may frequently trip over objects. They may have difficulty with anticipatory movements such as in catching a ball.

Poor sensory integration of the vestibular/ proprioceptive system can also impact on an individual's **posture and muscle tone, eye muscle control, and visual perceptual** development. This can interfere with the ability to maintain an appropriate sitting posture, copy from the blackboard, learn letters and numbers, organize work materials, and develop academic skills in language and math. If an individual's muscle tone is low, it interferes with energy levels, as well as motor skills. Handwriting can become very fatiguing in attempts to utilize an efficient grasp.

The inability to **regulate** or **modulate** sensation is another area of sensory integration dysfunction. When an individual cannot modulate sensory information an atypical reaction is usually seen. He/she may under react or over react to stimuli. For example, an individual who does not modulate vestibular (movement) information may continually seek movement to an intense degree. This person may seem to be in perpetual motion and unable to sit still. This creates problems in classrooms, restaurants, places of religious worship, and so on. At the opposite end of the spectrum a person may be extremely fearful of movement and avoid it at all costs.

A specific modulation disorder of sensory processing is **sensory defensiveness**. This is a neurologically based, unusually aversive reaction to sensory stimuli, which is not typically considered noxious. It is a difficulty in modulating sensory information. Sensory defensiveness can be present to just one, or to several areas of sensation. An individual can be defensive to touch or tactile sensations, auditory sensations, movement sensations, visual sensations, and olfactory sensations. Sensory defensiveness interferes with many aspects of life. Exposure to these sensations can cause distractibility, irritability, and increase stress levels tremendously.

Tactile defensive people often have trouble tolerating the touch of people near them, are very particular about the feel of certain clothing and food textures, often avoid engaging in any play activities such as sand, glue, paints, or variously textured toys, and have greater than average difficulty tolerating activities such as haircuts, nail cutting, and dental work.

Auditory defensiveness can interfere with tolerating noisy environments such as parties, cafeterias, gyms, and buses. It can make it difficult to follow verbal directions, and to learn and communicate through listening. Fire drills and other sudden loud sounds can be terrifying.

Movement hypersensitivity is called gravitational insecurity. This extreme fear of movement can interfere with any movement activities such as in the playground, gym, park, or sporting events.

Visual defensiveness can cause an individual to avoid bright lights, eye contact, and busily decorated rooms, and interfere with visual perceptual skills.

Olfactory defensiveness usually creates a very picky eater who would experience stress dealing with the everyday smells such as cooking food, perfumes, and pets. Many individuals with olfactory defensiveness cannot tolerate public restrooms or cafeterias. Sensory defensiveness takes many forms but always results in increased *stress* and difficulty in everyday life tasks.

Sensory integration dysfunction is usually evaluated by an occupational therapist. Many are certified in the interpretation and administration of the Sensory Integration and Praxis Test (SIPT). Treatment consists of specifically prescribed activities designed to assist in the integration of the various sensory systems, compensation techniques to help integrate sensory information on a daily basis, home program activities for carryover of treatment, and modifications to home, workplace, or classroom to help the individual adapt to sensory demands.

SENSORY MODULATION DYSFUNCTION

All people have different strategies for getting themselves to an appropriate level of alertness, and maintaining that level of alertness, so that they can attend and function in the tasks they want and have to do. Many of these strategies are the results of their **sensory needs.** People are able to work, play, rest, learn, and perform tasks when they are able to modulate their senses. Sensory modulation is the ability of the nervous system to monitor and regulate its own responses to the environment.

Some individuals have a sensory integration disorder called **poor sensory modulation or sensory modulation dysfunction.** This means that the nervous system has difficulty reacting efficiently and appropriately to sensory information that the body receives. This can interfere with comfort level, attention, learning styles, organization, and behavior.

An individual with sensory modulation dysfunction can present many different behaviors that are all part of the same condition. Some people may be highly sensitive and/or react aversively to sensory stimulation that is not typically considered noxious. This is hypersensitivity or sensory defensiveness. They may become agitated and extremely uncomfortable when exposed to sensory stimuli. Some individuals demonstrate sensory avoidance due to a milder sensory defensiveness. Here, the individual will not become as irritated, but may show some signs of distress, very specific sensory preferences, and avoidance patterns.

Some individuals have a milder sensitivity to sensory stimuli, but will still be able to continue their activities with less of an impact on their daily life. An individual can also be underresponsive or hyposensitive to sensory stimuli as well. Both hypersensitive and hyposensitive conditions can be present in the same person. It is also quite common for a person with sensory modulation problems to swing from hypersensitive to hyposensitive and rarely spend much time in the middle "typical" range. A person with sensory modulation difficulties may also need more time than average to process sensory information, and may therefore seem slow to respond and/or slow to calm down and reorganize themselves. The environment and activities of the day also influence the intensity of an individual's reaction to sensory input.

All sensory systems can be involved in this disorder, but it is more common to have several but not all of the systems involved. The sensory systems are **tactile** (sense of touch), **vestibular** (sense of movement), **proprioceptive** (joint and muscle sense), **auditory** (hearing), **visual** (seeing), **olfactory** (smell), and **gustatory** (taste). The following paragraphs discuss some possible signs and symptoms of poor sensory modulation in each system.

The **VESTIBULAR SYSTEM** is the system that tells us about movement in relationship to gravity. The **PROPRIOCEPTIVE SYSTEM** tells us how our muscles and joints are moving (how fast, with what force, in what direction). The vestibular and proprioceptive systems work together hand in hand. Poor modulation of the vestibular/proprioceptive systems can take several forms. An individual can be oversensitive to movement and become very fearful in situations where the feet leave the ground. Climbing, playground equipment, rides, or rough housing activities can be painful experiences. Sometimes motion sickness is also present. Some people may experience excessive nausea, dizziness, sweating, or increased heart rate in response to movement that would not typically cause such an extreme physical response. These people avoid movement activities and remain sedentary.

When an individual is under responsive to vestibular stimuli they seem to be in constant motion. They continually seek movement experiences and seem to take excessive movement risks without safety awareness. These are children who can't sit still in class and continually need to rock back on their chairs, tap their feet and hands, or flick at objects constantly. They are children who need more than the average vestibular input to maintain their appropriate level of alertness. Proprioceptive inefficiency can take the form of proprioceptive seeking activities such as toe walking, slapping feet, and pushing hard against surfaces to an inappropriate degree. Poor awareness of body in space and clumsiness also suggest proprioceptive inefficiency.

The **TACTILE SYSTEM** is the sensory system that tells us about touch. This system tells us first that we are being touched (protective system), and second, what is touching us (discriminatory system). It also helps to tell us what is safe and good, versus what is harmful. The balance of these two functions becomes disrupted in tactile modulation disorders.

A person who is tactile defensive is overly sensitive to touch sensations. He/she will react aversively to touch sensations that are not typically considered noxious. They may be overly sensitive to a variety of touch sensations such as a hand on the shoulder or head, personal hygiene activities such as combing hair or washing face/hands, or wearing certain types of clothing. They may feel very uncomfortable standing on lines or touching textures such as sand, glue, finger paints, or fuzzy sweaters. They might react aggressively when they feel threatened by simple touch experiences. The oral system could also be affected; the individual may be very sensitive to food textures or temperature and become a very "picky" eater.

The individual who is under reactive to tactile stimuli tends to be unaware of touch. They might seem stoic or unaware of pain as well. These people may bite or hit themselves. It is important to clearly identify this disorder. An individual who is highly sensitive could "shut down" his/her sensory system and appear unresponsive when they are actually extremely sensitive.

The **AUDITORY SYSTEM** is the sense of hearing. Individuals who are highly sensitive to auditory stimuli may be auditory defensive. These individuals may find sounds very distracting or irritating. They may become agitated by the sounds of beepers, watches, fans, or fluorescent lights. Noisy rooms such as indoor swimming pools, cafeterias, or gymnasiums can be very stressful. Difficulty paying attention or following directions can occur due to auditory defensiveness. Some children talk excessively or make their own sounds to help dampen the sound input they receive from the environment that they cannot control. Under responsive auditory systems cause an individual to be less responsive to sounds. This must be carefully ruled out from actual hearing loss.

The **VISUAL SYSTEM** is our sight system. An individual who is visually defensive may become stressed or overwhelmed in the presence of bright lights, busy environments, bright colors, sunshine, or a changing visual environment. Jewelry or busy classrooms may be difficult to tolerate. Many individuals who are visually defensive may avoid eye contact. An under-responsive visual system might cause poor focus and visual attention.

The **OLFACTORY SYSTEM** is a highly sensitive system and is generally an alerting system for the body. Individuals who are hypersensitive to smells may have a difficult time dealing with perfumes, food odors, and room odors. Many cannot tolerate public restrooms. They are often picky eaters. If they also have some defensiveness to tastes (gustatory) and/or tactile then food choices may be very limited. Smells are highly charged emotionally and may result in strong reactions.

Sensory modulation difficulties can also impact on behavior and comfort levels for an individual. They can interfere with a child's development because they can prevent exploration and trial and error activities. They keep an individual "on the defense" all the time, so that arousal levels remain higher than average. This may cause aggressive, explosive, stubborn, or uncooperative behaviors. This person may be continually trying to prevent situations where they may become overwhelmed or agitated. This can lead to controlling behaviors and takes a great deal of energy. Yet, sleep problems are common. A child who has sensory modulation difficulties has a hard time settling to sleep because they cannot change their alertness level easily. Consequently, falling asleep is a trying task.

Sensory modulation disorders can take many forms and presentations. It is imperative that an occupational therapist who understands sensory processing, works with the individual and family to evaluate and treat this condition.

ENVIRONMENTS AND THEIR SENSORY IMPACT

One way to help understand your child's sensory needs is to look at the different environments in which we all spend some time. Environments impact on our moods, stress levels, and even our behaviors. We might find ourselves calm and relaxed in a softly lit romantic restaurant or resting in a hammock on the beach. On the contrary, we may be much more excited, happy, or even agitated at a sporting event when the game is close, exciting, or when the outcome is very important to us. We would most likely agree that noisy environments impact on us quite differently than quiet ones. This section is designed to do part of what occupational therapists call an activity analysis of the different environments in which we find our children and ourselves. Evaluate every environment by the sensory aspects of it. Then, you can start to identify the assistance or hindrance it may provide your child.

In addition, each section contains some general concepts regarding the impact of different types of sensation in the environment, and how they impact on individuals. This is a generalized guideline and it is important to note that every child is unique. Not all of the generalizations will apply to your child.

THE VISUAL ENVIRONMENT

The visual environment is what we see as well as

what we don't see. Look at the order of the room. Does it have a lot of clutter or is everything in an orderly place? Are the colors bright or pastel, dark or light, patterned or non-patterned, and what are the colors seen? Are there sharp contrasts to the colors or are they blended smoothly? How many objects or distractions are there to be seen? Are the lines of the room or objects in the room sharp or curved? Are there a lot of moving objects or people and how fast is the movement? Are the lights dim or bright; are they fluorescent, full spectrum, or incandescent? What are the spatial elements like; are there many objects in view?

In general, dimmer lights, pastel or cool colors, orderly rooms, soft curves, soft contrasts, fewer objects to be seen, and visual movement that is slow and predictable tend to have a more calming influence on the nervous system. The opposite is true of bright or hot colors, clutter, sharp contrast, fast and irregular visual movement of objects, bright lights and fluorescent lights, and highly patterned images.

THE AUDITORY ENVIRONMENT

The auditory environment refers to the kinds of sounds we hear and do not hear. Is there a lot of background noise to ignore? How loud are the sounds? What kind of sounds can be heard- music, talking, mechanical noises, outside noises, white noise, etc. Be aware of subtle noises made by fans, blinds, heaters, blowing air, and the fluorescent lights. What about the echo from sounds-especially in indoor pools or restrooms (flushing toilets). We are used to so many routine sounds that we often do not even notice them, but a child with auditory defensiveness may hear and notice them all too well. Lawnmowers, beepers, cell phones, alarm clocks, TV, dishwashers and numerous other conveniences bombard us every day. What type of music does your child prefer to listen to and to sing? What kinds of sounds does your child make?

We always alert to sound but we learn to habituate to familiar or continual ones. In general, soft, predictable, and routine sounds are more calming. Sudden or unexpected sounds, loud sounds, and irregular sounds are all alerting to us. Music has a varied impact on all people and there are many styles of music to please all tastes. We can use music to calm or alert us. Music has so much to offer, and many children have responded beautifully to the use of music in therapy and in everyday tasks.

THE TACTILE OR TOUCH ENVIRONMENT

The tactile environment refers to things we touch, as well as what touches us. Temperature will also be included here. What materials are used in your child's clothing, bedding, and towels and what are your child's preferences as to fabric? How does your child respond to hygiene materials such as soap, shampoo, paper towels, tissues, and the feel of water? What water temperature is preferred in the bath or shower? What rugs or chairs are in the environment, and how hard or soft are they? What toys are available for play, and what are the textures? Are there choices for varied textures such as smooth, rough, scratchy, or slippery? Are there pets and people in the room? Is there a lot of space available between people? Do individuals in the environment touch the child with a light touch or deep pressure touch?

In general terms, rough or scratchy textures, irregular shapes, sharp edges, crowded environments, and very hot or very cold temperatures tend to alert us. Light touch, such as tousling hair, or poking touch tends to alert us as well. We naturally protect our abdominal area (stomach), our face, and the bottoms of our feet because these places tend to be more sensitive to touch. Unexpected or unpredictable touch is highly alerting. We calm more easily to firm pressure touch (such as in a massage) and to broad areas touched rather than a poking touch. Neutral warmth is the warmth from our own bodies as if wrapped in blankets. That is also a calming temperature. Smooth textures, predictability of touch, regularity of shape, and softer fabrics tend to be more calming.

The mouth is an area very sensitive to texture. This is called oral tactile. Foods with multiple textures, such as soup or rocky mountain ice cream tend to alert the mouth and make the oral structures work harder. Crunchy textures tend to be alerting. Smooth textures and one-dimensional textures are more calming. Sucking tends to provide deep pressure and proprioception to the mouth, which is also calming and organizing. We are all familiar with the soothing that occurs with bottle, pacifier, and thumb sucking. Chewing "resistive" foods such as gum, bagels, fruit leathers, or meats also provides a similar input, but is more challenging to the muscles and structures of the mouth. Sensations of rough, scratchy, sharp, irregular shapes, spicy, salty, and extremes of temperature are alerting in the mouth. Sensations of smooth, creamy, melting, regularity of shape, bland, and neutral temperatures tend to be calming in the mouth.

THE OLFACTORY OR SMELL ENVIRONMENT

Scents and odors surround us daily. Take notice of which scents your child is breathing in the different environments. The smells of cleansers, air fresheners, cologne, body toiletries, cooking, craft activities (i.e. paste, glue), or even plants or flowers in a room may all have an impact on comfort levels.

Our sense of smell is very unique. We always alert to new smells; our bodies are "wired" to do so. Our physical and emotional response to the smell will dictate our reaction to it. Every person is different as to scent preferences and there are many strong emotional connections with smell for each individual. Much of what we prefer is developed by our experiences. How do you feel about the smell of smoke, the smell of a baby just out of the bath, the smell of your partner's cologne, or the smell of rotten eggs? Some scents seem to be more universal and some are entirely specific to each individual. Cologne companies spend a great deal of money trying to find the most popular scents. Aromatherapy has been developed into an entire specialty field. What can you learn about your child's unique responses and preferences to smell?

Strategies for using scent, therefore, are harder to generalize. Some common thoughts are that mint and citrus scents tend to be invigorating or revitalizing (hence more alerting). Vanilla, rose, and lavender are felt to be more relaxing or calming. Pine is considered a mood elevator. You can develop a calming association to certain scents by coupling a specific scent with another soothing activity. For example, always use the same vanilla scent when you bathe your child (if bathing is a soothing event). This may help your child learn to feel relaxed when exposed to that particular scent. You can also provide scents that you know are already associated with the feeling you want to evoke.

THE VESTIBULAR/PROPRIOCEPTIVE OR MOVEMENT ENVIRONMENT

Movement plays a big role in our ability to modulate our senses. Many children have difficulty getting just the right amount of movement they need. What opportunities does your child have to move throughout the day? Is it enough, or too much? Is it too little? What type of movement is available? Are there opportunities for proprioceptive input in the environment? The need and availability varies greatly depending on age and your child's needs. Most preschool and primary grades have playgrounds available during recess that allows for many movement opportunities. Playgrounds provide swings, seesaws, gliders, and spinning rides to provide vestibular input, and they include climbing, digging, and jumping equipment to provide proprioceptive input. As children enter middle school and high school, however, this is clearly decreased. Physical education classes provide structured movement opportunities for these students, but much of it is dependent on a higher level of motor skill. They may not provide enough intensity of stimuli for some students with special sensory processing needs. What alternate movement activities are available to your child?

Slow, regular, linear, and predictable movement tends to be calming. Children with sensitivity to movement thrive on this type of movement. Many children who seek movement need this type of input to calm. Movement that is unpredictable, fast, irregular, and rotary tends to be stimulating. Some children need more movement than average to feel calm and organized. Proprioceptive input is gained through "heavy work" of the muscles and joints, such as in pushing, pulling, climbing, lifting heavy objects, moving the body through resistive activities, or intense repetitive exercise. This input is also gained in stretching the muscles and joints. Proprioceptive input is generally calming and organizing to the nervous system.

PARENT RESOURCES

BOOKS/PUBLICATIONS

The Hidden Senses: Your Balance Sense by Jane Koomar and Barbara Friedman
The Hidden Senses: Your Muscle Sense by Jane Koomar and Barbara Friedman
Published by PDP Press
www.pdppress.com
These books are written for children to explain the vestibular and proprioceptive systems and how they function in our bodies.

Secrets of the Baby Whisperer   by   Tracy Hogg
Secrets of the Baby Whisperer for Toddlers by Tracy Hogg
Published by: Ballantine Publishing
www.ballantinebooks.com
These are not books regarding sensory integration but the author discusses methods to calm and communicate with your child. She has a unique presentation.

The Explosive Child by Ross W. Greene
Published by Harper Collins Publishers- Quill
www.harpercollins.com
This book is a behavioral approach to helping children with noncompliant and explosive behaviors. It is not about sensory integration.

The Out of Sync Child by Carol Stock Kranowitz
Published by Perigree Books

The Out of Sync Child Has Fun by Carol Stock Kranowitz
Published by Perigree Books
www.penguinputnam.com
www.outofsyncchild.com
These books specifically deal with sensory integration and provide many activity ideas for kids of all abilities.

Raising Your Spirited Child by Mary Sheedy Kurcinka
Published by Harper Collins
www.harpercollins.com
This is not a book that even mentions sensory integration but you may find your SI child hidden inside its covers. The author writes in a sensitive and caring manner.

The Challenging Child by Stanley I. Greenspan
Published by Perseus Books
www.perseuspublishing.com
Dr. Greenspan is well known for his interventions with children with special needs. He has included sensory integration concepts into much of his work.

Sleep Better- A Guide to Improving Sleep for Children with Special Needs by V. Mark Durand
Published by Paul H. Brooks Publishing
www.brookespublishing.com
This book explores the many sleep problems encountered by children with special needs and offers ideas and solutions for them.

SI and the Child – 25th Anniversary Edition by A. Jean Ayres
Published by Western Psychological Services
www.Slfocus.com
The original parent book by Dr. Ayres herself. This new

version is revised and Edited by Pediatric Therapy Network

The Mozart Effect for Children by Don Campbell
Published by William Morrow Publishing
www.harpercollins.com
www.MozaertEffect.com
Don Campbell uses music in creative and inspiring ways and explains how music affects your child.

The Highly Sensitive Child by Elaine N. Aron, Ph.D
Published by Broadway Books
www.broadwaybooks.com
This book does not discuss sensory integration but discusses the emotional aspects of children who are sensitive both in physical and emotional areas. It gives many practical suggestions for communication and parenting.

Too Loud, Too Bright, Too Fast, Too Tight by Sharon Heller, Ph.D.
Published by HarperCollins Publishers
www.harpercollins.com
This book was written by a woman who is sensory defensive and offers numerous insights and suggestions. It is geared more towards adults but is quite helpful for parents of children with sensory defensiveness.

S.I Focus Magazine
www.SIfocus.com
This is a magazine that provides current information regarding sensory integration, through articles by both parents and professionals.

Sensory Defensiveness in Children Aged 2-12 by Patricia and

Julia Wilbarger
Published by PDP Press
www.pdppress.com
This pamphlet describes sensory defensiveness. It was written by the creators of the Wilbarger Protocol. This protocol is commonly referred to as pressure brushing.

Quirky Kids by Perri Klass, MD and Eileen Costello, MD
www.ballantinebooks.com
This book, written by pediatricians, helps to illuminate the many terms and diagnoses given to children and addresses ideas for many common questions such as family life, school, medications, and therapies. They do discuss sensory integration.

Asperger Syndrome and Sensory Issues by Myles, Tapscott
Cook, Miller, Rinner, and Robbins
Published by Autism Asperger Publishing CO.
www.asperger.net
This book describes the sensory problems seen in children with Asperger Syndrome with some practical suggestions.

The Sensory Sensitive Child by Karen A. Smith and Karen R. Gouze
Published by Harper Resource
www.harpercollins.com
This book was written by two practicing psychologists who are also parents of children with sensory integration problems

CATALOGS/SUPPLIES:

Southpaw Enterprises: 1-800-228-1698
www.southpawenterprises.com
Sensory integration equipment for home and clinic

Free Spirit Publishing: 1-800-735-7323
www.freespiritpublishing.com
Books for and about kids with learning challenges

FlagHouse: 1-800-793-7900
www.FlagHouse.com
Equipment for gross and fine motor skills, sensory integration equipment

Sensory Comfort: 1-888-436-2622
www.sensorycomfort.com
Clothing and articles for individuals with sensory processing challenges

Sport Time Abilitations: 1-800-850-8602
www.abilitations.com
Equipment for gross and fine motor skills, sensory integration equipment

Therapro 1-800-257-5376
www.theraproducts.com
Equipment for gross and fine motor skills, perceptual motor development

Sensory Resources 1-888-357-5867
www.SensoryResources.com
Sensory integration and motor equipment

PDP Press 651-439-8865
www.pdppress.com
Sensory integration equipment, books, videos

Achievement Products 1-800-373-4699
www.specialkidszone.com
Equipment for motor and sensory development

Pocket Full of Therapy 1-800-PFOT-124
www.pfot.com
Sensory and motor equipment, perceptual motor equipment

Therafin 1-800-843-7234
www.therafin.com
Providers of the "squeeze machine" developed by Temple Grandin

AlphaSmart, Inc. 888-274-0680
www.alphasmart.com
Table top typing device with screen

Beyond Play 1-877-428-1244
www.beyondplay.com
Early Intervention products for children with special needs

ORGANIZATIONS and HELPFUL WEBSITES:

American Occupational Therapy Association
www.aota.org

Advanced Brain Technologies
www.advancedbrain.com

Vital Links
www.vitallinks.net

Sensory Integration Network
www.sinetwork.com

American Academy of Audiology
www.audiology.org

American Speech –Language -and Hearing Association
www.asha.org

National Coalition on Auditor y Processing Disorders
www.ncapd.org

LD Newsletter Online
www.ldonline.org

COMMUNICATE
Step Two

COMMUNICATION WITH YOUR CHILD

Children with sensory modulation dysfunction do not always understand why they act or feel the way they do. Let your child know that we all process sensory information differently and that we all do things in our own way to help us pay attention and organize our behavior. Explain some of the things you do to help yourself. For example, you may explain that you really like to shower in the morning to help you become alert and ready to work; or that you like to listen to quiet music or have a warm cup of tea at night to help you feel calm. Maybe you chew gum when you have to concentrate, or maybe you can only work in a quiet room. Point out the activities that you see your child do that you think might be modulating him. For example, you may say that you notice that your child can pay better attention to homework after completing some exercise.

It is important to let your child understand that some of the ways to modulate are more efficient than others, and some are more appropriate than others. Help your child find appropriate ways to deal with sensory needs and emotional/behavioral needs. Say, for example, your tactile defensive child hits a boy in school who accidentally brushed against your child's arm. You may explain that while you understand that it felt like the boy was hurting your child, hitting him was probably not the best choice of reaction. "What else could you have done?" Offer choices if your child cannot think of any. "Maybe you could have walked away, used your words, or pressed hard on the spot that hurt you to make you feel better."

Try to communicate to your child that you want to understand and help. Questions such as "What do you need to help you feel better?" or "What can I do to help you calm down?" communicate that you are "on the same team." Provide suggestions that you know will help your child. "Let's try to play some music; let's try wrapping up in a blanket; let's try chewing some gum," are ways to offer suggestions that are helpful to your child and teach self regulating strategies. Try to find out what about a particular event or object is so disturbing to your child. Ask open ended, but specific questions such as, "What is it about this shirt that bothers you so much? Where does the shirt irritate you? Do you like the sleeves long or short? Does the fabric feel good or bad?" and so on. It may take many questions to get to the heart of the matter, but this will give you much insight into your child's sensory processing. It will also begin to give your child tools to communicate with you and others. Even a few simple words can empower your child. Look for patterns in the answers to many questions over many events.

Model and communicate what you do regarding the sensory strategies you use. You may want to spend some time analyzing your own sensory system, as well as other significant family members, to see how they all fit together. This will help all of you to learn so much more about each other. More obvious things, such as who likes spicy food and who likes bland food, are easy to start. You may also want to notice who seems to like the TV or radio louder or softer than others, who seems to prefer certain fabrics in clothing or bed sheets, or who is the first one to notice a visual change in the environment. You also want to note what others do to help them modulate their sensory systems to pay attention, organize their behavior, stay calm, and do work. We are all different and all use different strategies. Helping your child and your whole family understand that concept will make life easier for your child with sensory modulation dysfunction. You might also want to look at any family strategies that are in competition with each other. For example, what can we do when Dad needs quiet to calm and settle at the same time Sister needs some alerting activities to engage in her homework?

Another important aspect of communication is non-verbal. Children can be very receptive and sensitive to this type of communication. This is the information you give your child by your body language, your facial expressions, and your general attitude. You can use this to help your child feel capable and confident. When you believe in your children, they will believe in themselves. When you feel calm, so will your child. When you expect your child to accomplish- he will. When you become anxious or negative, your child will pick up on these emotions as well. This may impact on behavior patterns. If you expect your child to refuse an activity and have a tantrum, you may inadvertently encourage that. So focus on the positive, and look to each little step you and your child travel. Keep focused on the "big picture" but remember to delight in the little accomplishments along the way.

COMMUNICATION WITH OTHERS

When speaking with others use simple explanations and communicate the strategies that are working. For example, you may need to tell grandma that if she waits a few minutes before seeking that delightful hug and kiss from her grandchild, she will get it with more enthusiasm. Sudden unpredictable hugs or kisses can be devastating for a tactile defensive child. With a little preparation and some control on the part of the child, the interaction can become enjoyable for all. You may need to tell the teacher that sitting near the fan is hard for your child to tolerate. When people see success in the strategies suggested, they are more likely to understand and cooperate. Modeling on your part is also essential. When babysitters, friends, or family see how you interact and make life more comfortable for your child, they are more likely to follow in your footsteps. Enlist the help of those people, professionals or otherwise, that understand your child when communicating with those who don't.

PARTICIPATE
Step Three

This section is the main purpose of this book. What can you do to help your child PARTICIPATE in all that life has to offer? And how can you make these events and experiences meaningful and pleasurable for your child who struggles with sensory integration dysfunction?

This unit of the book is divided into sections that speak to the differing presentations of sensory integration dysfunction. These are divided into the following categories:

■ The Clumsy Child: The child with Dyspraxia

■ The Disorganized Child: The child with Central Vestibular/Proprioceptive Processing Dysfunction:

■ The Sensitive Child: The child with Sensory Modulation Dysfunction

For each presentation, an overview of that specific set of behaviors is described. A story is told that describes a day in the life of a child who presents with each type of sensory processing inefficiency, and the same story retold with strategies put into place. A list of suggestions for children is also provided.

The suggestions in this book may not ALL be appropriate for ALL children. It is your job, as a parent, to make sense of these suggestions for your child and family. It is also important to consult with your OT or other professional helping your child. They can help you put the details of these ideas into place.

THE CLUMSY CHILD

❖

THE CHILD WITH DYSPRAXIA

THE CLUMSY CHILD:
A DAY IN THE LIFE OF A CHILD
WITH DYSPRAXIA

This is a fictional account of a very real problem. While David's day and David do not exist, many children experience days, or parts of days, like this all the time. You might recognize someone you know.

David is a child with dyspraxia in a mainstream third grade classroom. As soon as he awakens in the morning, his mom tells him to get dressed. This is very difficult for him because of his motor planning problems. He has trouble getting his shirt in the right direction, donning the sleeves the right way, and getting his legs into the pants. Finally, he accomplishes this task. When he is finished, he descends the stairs, stomping his feet on the steps as he tries to get some proprioceptive feedback. His mom hushes him saying, "Quiet! You'll wake up your sister." In the kitchen, he opens the brand new box of cereal, ripping the entire box top off, sending cereal flying across the room and onto the floor. When he pours the milk on the cereal that did manage to get into the bowl, he can't grade his movements appropriately, and the milk overflows the bowl. "Hurry, hurry!" his mom rushes him; he takes so long that he will miss the bus.

David finally makes it to school, and unloading his backpack proves to be a struggle. He takes much longer than the other children. All of the other students are in their seats, and David is still struggling to keep up. As the children begin their morning journal, they have to copy the "question of the day" off of the chalkboard. David continues to struggle with his handwriting and organization. He doesn't know where to put the date and where to start in his notebook. He presses so hard with the pencil that his hand hurts, he breaks the point of the pencil, and has to get out of his seat to sharpen it. On the way to the sharpener, he trips on the leg of a student's chair. Finally, back at his seat, he has trouble holding the pencil in an appropriate grip, forming the letters correctly, and he occasionally drops his pencil to the floor. David works so hard to organize his body and motor skills that he barely has time or energy to answer the question despite all of the thoughts he has in his head. "Time's up!" announces the teacher, and the students are invited to share their answers with the class. David slouches in his seat feeling frustrated and embarrassed. When he is called on he verbally describes the ideas in his head, none of which are on the paper.

Now, it's project time. The class is making butterflies. They have to color the picture, cut it out, and glue it. David has difficulty coloring in the lines, and then cutting with the scissors. When he squeezes the glue, it comes out in a huge puddle. David tries to put the pieces of the butterfly together. He knows exactly how it should look, but he can't figure out how to make it happen.

Finally, it's silent reading time. David has a few minutes of peace, as he loves to read and enjoys his favorite time of the day. This peace doesn't last long, however because it is soon lunchtime. The children rush to their lunch boxes and to get on the lunch line. David tries his best, without much success, to keep the pace. Today he is buying lunch, but he almost drops his tray, and he can't open the milk carton. He's sloppy when he eats, and the kids tease him about the food on his face and lap. At recess, he avoids playing soccer with the boys; he's pretty good at dribbling, but he can't do it in a game with the constant changes and the other children to move around. He avoids climbing on the playground monkey bars because he can't sequence his movements to be successful. Most of recess is spent watching from the sidelines. He doesn't have many friends.

After lunch, it's time for math, another one of David's enjoyable subjects. But, when he has to tear the perforated pages off the book, he rips off several problems, and can't complete the page.

David's next challenge is gym. It takes more time for him to change his clothing, and he runs out of the locker room with his shoes untied. Tying shoes poses another challenge. He cannot tie his shoes without carefully watching each and every step of the way. He needs to visually monitor his motor actions. The other challenge he faces in gym is the combination lock. He never seems to get those numbers to line up correctly. David is disciplined in gym very often. He's always talking and trying to change the games. He does this to avoid embarrassment because he knows what to do and the rules of the games, but he just can't make his body perform those actions. Distraction and trying to control the game are strategies he uses to take attention from his lack of skills.

Finally, it's time to go home. The rush is on as children pack up their belongings, copy their homework off the chalkboard, and put on their coats. David is very slow to copy his homework, so he doesn't get to write it all down.

What he does manage to scribble down is so illegible that he isn't able to read it when he gets home. The zipper on his backpack jams and he has no clue how to fix it. He tries to jam the books he needs through the limited opening and is able to get most of them in, but in his struggles, he misses a few important items. His desk is quite disorderly which compounds the frustrations. David runs to the bus line and slumps in his seat. He is too tired and frustrated to talk to the other students. Who has energy for social skills? David's self-esteem is very low.

David arrives home. Now it is time for the dreaded homework. More handwriting struggles, more frustration with not having all of the information written down in his agenda, and the problem of not having all of the materials he needs because he was not able to bring them home. David's mom was pleased to tell him that he got an invitation in the mail to a birthday party- a bowling party. David does not want to go. Why? Because he avoids new situations that may challenge his motor planning and make him feel embarrassed. All he wants to do right now is watch television.

SIGNS AND SYMPTOMS OF DYSPRAXIA

Dyspraxia is often called poor motor planning. It stems primarily from deficits in processing information from the tactile (specifically discriminatory functions) and proprioceptive systems. A child with somatodyspraxia has trouble figuring out how to use his/her body or to use tools in novel ways. This child may take longer and struggle harder to learn new tasks than the typical child and he may be less able to change already learned tasks. Each change in a task requires praxis (motor planning) all over again. What are some of the challenges a child with dyspraxia may face?

Following is a checklist of the kinds of problems you may see. Not all children will have trouble in all of these areas. Children may exhibit some of these, but not necessarily all of them.

MOTOR PERFORMANCE

- Appears clumsy and often trips

- Drops pencils, books, papers, toys, or has difficulty carrying objects

- Has difficulty getting objects out of toy box, backpacks, desks, lunch boxes, lockers

- Slaps feet while walking, toe walks, or sit hard into seats

- Needs to visually monitor motor actions to gain additional information; can't do something motor without using eyes to help, for example, tie shoes

- Has difficulty in, and dislikes/avoids physical education class, playground activities, sports, or motor activities; this child may learn motor skills in isolation but has difficulty incorporating these skills into a game situation. (ex. may be able to dribble a soccer ball but can't dribble around opponents and change directions through the game)

- Won't enjoy or explore playground; has a lack of strategies to explore; may play on equipment in familiar rote routines rather than try new adaptive strategies

- Poor fine motor skills such as cutting, pasting (squeezes glue too hard), coloring (difficulty staying in lines), printing; lacks appropriate pressure on objects due to lack of proprioceptive integration; may be inadvertently destructive with toys.

- Difficulty in Technology classes, Home and Careers, and Art classes due to fine motor and motor planning deficits

- Difficulty tearing out perforated pages in workbooks

- SLOW to move or takes longer to perform a motor task; takes longer in school to get on line, put away coat and books, etc; this is due to the extra time needed to motor plan

- Knows where to place a puzzle piece, but cannot figure out how to fit it into the space; this occurs when visual spatial or perceptual skills are intact. The child sees what to do but cannot figure out how to make his or her body do it.

- Has poor or delayed self care skills; this child may have difficulty donning and doffing clothing in a timely fashion, figuring out how to brush teeth or comb hair, change for physical education in time for class; tying shoes, operating fasteners, etc.

- Difficulty operating a combination lock and locker, turning doorknobs, or using a key

- Difficulty carrying cafeteria trays, pouring milk, cutting food, opening packages, and may appear to be a sloppy eater

ORGANIZATION/ACADEMIC

- Poorly organized, poor sequencing and timing, difficulty following routines

- Appears messy at desk or lunchroom or keep personal belongings messy or disorganized

- Difficulty arranging paper headings, writing in columns, folding paper, writing in small spaces

- May forget to bring home, or to classes, correct papers, books, homework

- May loose things easily

What appears to be forgetfulness in the child with dyspraxia may not be due to memory deficits, but it may be related to difficulty organizing thoughts and actions. It may also be due to the time restraints children in school have to quickly get their belongings together for dismissal or changing classes. A dyspraxic child may need more time than given to get all items together as needed. The energy expenditure is also great which impacts on ability to remember all items.

HANDWRITING

- Learning to draw shapes, print, or write may be difficult. Changing writing methods may also be difficult. Asking a child to write on a different type of paper than the one accustomed to, or to write in a designated shape may also be quite challenging.

- Presses hard on pencil, break tips on points

- Awkward, inconsistent grip on writing and eating utensils; delay in developing grasp patterns.

- Poor letter formation

- Poor ability to copy and to print spontaneously

SOCIAL EMOTIONAL BEHAVIORS

The behaviors described below are some ways that children with dyspraxia may try to compensate for the deficits described above. Behavior is a complicated matter, and this list is just intended to give some possibilities that are related to sensory integration problems.

- Avoids difficult tasks by talking instead of doing

- Become frustrated because child may see what he/she cannot accomplish

- Tries to manipulate situations to avoid stressful or embarrassing situations

- Avoids new situations or has difficulty in transitions

- Has low self esteem

STRATEGIES TO HELP THE CLUMSY CHILD

DYSPRAXIA

Strategies for the child with DYSPRAXIA involve providing appropriate sensory information, minimizing the motor stressors, providing organizational systems, and providing information for understanding.

MOTOR PERFORMANCE/SELF CARE SKILLS

- Keep aisles between the school desks wide, and seat the child where he/she will have less distance or obstacles to motor plan around. Minimize clutter in aisles.

- Put toppers on pencils to avoid having them roll off the desk and across the floor if dropped. A piece of loop velcro wrapped around a pencil which can be attached to a piece of hook velcro on the desk provides a stable pencil holder. Reusable putty adhesive also provides a pencil holder.

- Choose clothing that is easy to change, ie. loose fitting, tube socks, velcro sneakers, etc.

- Minimize amount of changing clothing for gym. For example, have your child come to school with gym shorts already under sweat pants and a T-shirt under the outer shirt.

- Use straight barrel lock instead of round combination lock. Key locks are usually difficult to manage because keys get lost so easily. Newer locks available have larger numbers and less rotation involved. Some are even shaped more "hand friendly."

- Provide extra storage at the side of the desk for books and papers so there is more space to find things quickly. Organize bedroom storage so that spaces are clearly marked or labeled to specify where items belong. Use words or pictures as needed.

- Provide easy open packages and lunchboxes for the cafeteria, use easy open boxes for school supplies in younger grades. Some parents start a small slit or opening in the package so that it is easier for the child to open. Practice with the backpacks and lunchboxes at home before they are brought to school.

- Make sure the scissors, pencils, and other tools are good effective tools. The erasers should be soft, pencils sharp, and scissors sharp but safe.

FINE MOTOR/HANDWRITING

- Many children with dyspraxia can use keyboarding and word processing on a computer to minimize the motor demands.

- Pencil grippers are usually helpful for this group of children. Rubber bands wrapped around the pencil make a successful gripper for older children who do not want to look different.

- It is often easier to learn handwriting in patterns of

movement, using similiar strokes as much as possible. For example, learning the straight line letters all together (I, T, H, E, F, L). Using language cues and mini stories to assist is very helpful. For example, the number 5's story is "a boy was walking down the street (straight line down); he turns the corner (round out the bottom curve); and his hat blows off (make the top line of the 5).

- Request that homework assignments such as writing spelling words ten times each, be minimized. These children do not usually learn by writing since all the cognitive energy is spent on the writing itself rather than the spelling. Request modification of the amount of written work. Tape recorded or oral presentation might be a good replacement for some writing if it is not too cumbersome.

- Discourage activities that require writing in small spaces, such as filling in small charts or graphs or writing sentences into predesigned shapes. The task may need to be modified by providing larger spaces, typing, or changing the design of the paper.

- Raised line paper provides an extra sensory cue for handwriting. For coloring, outline the picture to color with colored or white glue to make a "frame" once it is dry. You can also use waxed string as an outline. These techniques also provide an extra sensory cue to stay within the lines.

- Use handwriting teaching methods that provide extra visual cues. For example, use colored lines for stop, start, and middle. You can color code the lines as a traffic light.

Make the top line green because green means "go" and that is where we start printing letters. The middle line is yellow to proceed with slow and careful lines. The bottom line is red to stop at the bottom. You can also provide boxes for letters, and dots for start and stop cues.

- Note taking is the most difficult area for handwriting problems. Lap top computer systems and other technology units are becoming more available and user friendly for this task. Teach your child to develop a good system of abbreviations and outlining to minimize writing. Teach highlighting skills in reading texts. Tape recorders are sometimes helpful but do require extra time at home to listen again. Teacher generated notes/outlines is another strategy that has frequently been helpful to students.

- Voice to text computer systems are becoming more available and inexpensive. They provide multiple advantages in addition to minimizing handwriting. Look carefully at the age of your child and the demands of the system. A user must have a consistent and clear voice pattern for the programs to work efficiently.

ACADEMICS/ORGANIZATION

- Provide structured routines that are written or drawn for younger children. This helps to "pre-organize" the child by letting him/her to know what is expected.

- Color code the books, notebooks, and binders with the same color for the same subjects. Keep the same colors year to year so, for example, green always means Science.

- Minimize the amount of books or objects a child needs to carry from place to place. For example, use 3 subject notebooks and binders with several folders together. Many notebooks have folder pockets built right in. Some children do better with one larger binder organized for several, or all, subjects.

- Looseleaf binders will need hole reinforcers on both sides of the paper because they rip so quickly with handling. There is a commercially available paper that is reinforced already.

- Arrange for your child to have an extra set of texts at home. This will most likely have to be written into the child's Individualized Education Plan and the need determined by the Committee for Special Education.

- Use electronic organizers for recording homework assignments. Some of these are quite complicated so this must be investigated carefully.

- Use calendars as early as possible to assist in developing organizational strategies. Keep a color coded schedule at home and school.

- Break tasks up into small units that can be successfully accomplished within a short period of time.

- Help organize math problems using graph paper; turn lined paper or looseleaf paper sideways to make columns.

- Use auditory cues to help learn spelling or memorize

information. For example, use rhythm or singing/music to spell words in musical pattern. Chanting with movement is also helpful. A phonics approach also uses significant auditory cues.

- Multisensory teaching methods such as writing in sand, fingerpaints, pudding, or other textures help to give extra sensory cues to assist in motor learning. Stroking the arm for each letter of a spelling word or tapping out the syllables is also helpful.

CLASSROOM AND HOME SENSORIMOTOR INTEGRATION ACTIVITIES FOR THE DYSPRAXIC CHILD

These are every day enjoyable activities that are based on sensory integration concepts to help improve sensory motor processing.

- Practice tearing perforated pages by tearing out coupons from the newspaper and magazines. Many children's activity books also have perforated pages for advanced practice.

- Soft leads (numbers higher than two) or weighted pencils are good for practice with handwriting. They provide additional sensory cues. Markers also provide additional sensation when writing and drawing.

- Provide "heavy work" activities that offer opportunities for enhanced sensory intake. These are activities that are resistive in nature, such as carrying heavy books, wearing a weighted backpack or weighted vest, moving chairs or other light furniture, and pushing a wagon or cart to assist teacher. Many teachers will have students use a wagon to get the milk for snack or send students to get the audiovisual cart. Fine motor and upper extremity "heavy work" can be provided through clay activities, erasing the chalkboard, hanging from a trapeze bar in the playground, and washing tables or desktops.

- Home chores such as raking, sweeping, vacuuming, digging, carrying "heavy objects," such as groceries or trash cans/bags are helpful.

- Cooking tasks that require using the arms and hands against resistance such as kneading dough, rolling with a rolling pin, and stirring stiff foods such as crisped rice cereal treats are excellent.

- Place paper to be colored over a piece of textured ceiling or lighting tile or soft window screen material. As the child colors, the texture creates an interesting pattern and also provides for enhanced sensory intake. Concrete sidewalks and cinderblock walls also provide a textured surface. Sidewalk chalk activities can also provide the same concept, on a larger scale, without paper.

- Vibrating pens for play activity is another way to provide enhanced sensory intake.

- Involve the child in activities that involve pushing, pulling, and climbing at his/her own pace. Climbing is an excellent activity to develop motor planning.

- Place waxed string or colored glue lines (let dry, of course) on a piece of paper between which the child can practice scissor cutting. Vary the width as appropriate to the child's skill.

- Practice cutting with scissors using manila file folders or thin cardboard inserts that may be found inside clothing packages, such as socks, pantyhose, or gloves. The stiffer material is easier to cut, and it provides additional sensory input to better feel the task.

- Children also love cutting stiff plastic straws. They tend to "fly" across the room with each snip.

A DAY IN THE LIFE OF DAVID: A CHILD WITH DYSPRAXIA (revisited)
The Clumsy Child

Remember David, the 3rd grader with dyspraxia? His parents and teachers put a few modifications into his day to minimize the stressors. Here is his new story.

As soon as he awakens in the morning, David does not get dressed right away. He begins a short exercise program of jumping jacks, pushing and pulling on a stretchy material called Theraband with his arms and his legs, and squeezing a squishy ball ten times with each hand. He then gets dressed more quickly as his body has just received proprioceptive and vestibular input to increase his awareness and motor planning. His mom laid out his clothes in the correct direction the night before, so he more easily slips into them. He doesn't need to stomp down the stairs as he has already received the input his body needed to get started. He uses a small pair of scissors kept near the cereal box to open it and pours from a smaller container kept in the refrigerator for him. Things go so smoothly that he has a few moments to jump again on the small exercise trampoline that is kept in his den.

At school, his teacher is now aware of his needs and gives him a few extra moments to get his belongings together. This also goes a little faster for him because he now uses a backpack that is easier to open. His teacher gives him the "question of the day" preprinted so that he does not have to waste time recopying the question and thus has more time to concentrate on his writing. He also uses a pencil grip that his OT provided to help him feel more comfortable and more consistent in his grasp pattern. He uses more efficient tools, sharper scissors and a glue stick, to make projects more manageable. He is happier at lunch because his mother makes sure that he has easy open packages. He has learned to do a few chair pushups and jumping activities before he plays motor games to give himself the sensory input he needs to organize his motor skills. He still struggles with team sports but, with help, he has learned the things that he is good at, and finds those activities that are rewarding to him. "We all have our strengths and weaknesses," he will say.

Homework challenges are also getting easier. He has learned to use the computer for lengthy assignments, and his teacher has modified the amount of written work she gives him to do. He uses verbal projects and answers for some of his work. He is able to bring home the items he needs, most of the time, because his teacher and OT have set up a take home checklist, a color coded system, and he has an extra set of texts at home.

Socially, David has a bit more energy for activities and parties. He joined a photography club and a runner's club in the community. He is meeting friends with similar interests.

David still faces daily challenges, but he tries to participate in "figuring out" what he needs to be successful. He is only in 3rd grade, but, he has made a good start to feeling in control of his world. He still needs the caring and educated adults in his world to help him with this process.

THE DISORGANIZED CHILD

❖

CENTRAL VESTIBULAR PROPRIOCEPTIVE PROCESSING DYSFUNCTION

THE DISORGANIZED CHILD: A DAY IN THE LIFE OF A CHILD WITH VESTIBULAR/PROPRIOCEPTIVE PROCESSING DYSFUNCTION

This is a fictional account of a very real problem. While Vicki and Vicki's day do not exist, many children experience many of these events all the time. Maybe you will recognize someone you know.

Vicki is a Kindergarten student with vestibular processing dysfunction. She starts her day getting dressed- or trying to. She has trouble with buttons and getting the clothes on in the right order. At breakfast, she tries to eat her cereal, but she neglects to hold the bowl as she scoops with the spoon. The bowl flies across the table. When she gets to school, she forgets the order of events- hang up the coats, put away the backpacks, place homework and notes from home in the box on the teacher's desk, and take out the notebooks. Her muscle tone is low, and she sits slumped in her chair as if she is tired. She is not tired, but feels embarrassed when her teacher asks her if she had gotten enough sleep. When she writes her letters, she holds her head in her hands and does not adjust her body to the desk. She still switches her hands as she moves across the paper. She uses the right hand on the right side of her body and the left hand on the left side of her body. She switches the pencil at the midline of her body. She never developed a good skilled hand with which to write, and her letters are often formed incorrectly. She often does not hold her paper down so her writing is even sloppier looking than it has to be. She fatigues easily when she writes, and she wraps her fingers around the pencil to get a good grip. She never seems to finish her class work because her hands get so tired. She gets distracted and fidgety too. It seems the longer she sits, the more she slumps in her chair, and her attention tends to drift. When she realizes that she is not paying attention, she starts to rock in her chair or tip it back on its hind legs. The teacher tells her she must sit still. She tries, but she just seems to need to move to pay attention.

Now it is time to go to gym. Vicki loves gym but always seems to get in trouble. Once she starts running and jumping she gets so silly that she just cannot stop. This happens to her in the playground as well, and she often loses her recess time because she "cannot control herself." Funny, but those days she seems to have even more trouble paying attention in the afternoon.

Vicki stays after school for a day care program. She loves it here. The teacher gives her a chewy snack, has a structured playtime that allows the students to move to music CDs, and they even have a piano in the room. Vicki feels so comfortable with the structured movement, and the music seems to organize her.

SIGNS AND SYMPTOMS OF THE CHILD WITH CENTRAL VESTIBULAR/PROPRIOCEPTIVE PROCESSING DEFICITS

Central vestibular/proprioceptive deficits are believed to be caused by an inefficient processing of the information received from the vestibular system (which is a highly specialized proprioceptor) as well as from the additional sources of proprioceptive information received through active movement of the head and body.

Children with central vestibular/proprioceptive processing deficits have difficulties in posture and movement, which impact on their ability to organize their bodies for optimal learning. They may have different needs regarding movement than the typical child. The vestibular system has a pervasive effect on many parts of the nervous system. It impacts on the visual system, the attention/arousal mechanisms, auditory system, and limbic system (the limbic system plays a role in emotions).

The following is a list of some of the challenges a child with Central Vestibular/Proprioceptive Dysfunction may encounter. Not all of the problems will be experienced by all of the children.

MOTOR/POSTURAL

- Low muscle tone influencing poor sitting and standing postures, for example, slumping in chair, head resting on hand when writing at desk

- Poor joint stability, may appear "weak"

- Poor grip patterns on utensils, for example excessive wrapping of fingers around object, or use of extra fingers to gain stability

- Poor body awareness and schema with mild motor planning deficits

- Poor balance and equilibrium in playground, may fall or trip when balance is challenged

- Feels heavy for his/her size due to low muscle tone

- May not naturally adjust body into positions that facilitate task at hand. For example, the child may not naturally lean forward in seat to eat or write or may not shift weight easily to catch a ball.

- Poor two handed task performance, such as use of scissors, lacing, stringing beads, shoe tying, snaps, buttons, zippers, opening milk carton, pouring, opening clasp binders, etc.

- Difficulty using the two sides of the body in a coordinated fashion, which impacts on the ability to balance and perform bilateral skills

- Poor bilateral gross motor skills such as jumping jacks, jumping with two feet together, carrying cafeteria tray, etc.

- Poor bilateral skills that require anticipation or

sequencing of movement such as catching a ball and kicking a rolling ball

- Tends to trip over or bump into moving objects, such as other children and balls in the playground

ORGANIZATION/ACADEMICS

- Poor eye muscle control

- Poor visual focus and visual attending

- Difficulty reading due to poor eye muscle control and focus

- Poor visual perception

- Poor midline orientation and midline crossing at tabletop; may need to move paper or objects to side or to move body to avoid crossing midline; sometimes will actually lean or fall right out of the seat to avoid crossing midline

- Difficulty in reading, math, and spelling due to sequencing and midline deficits; may miss the middle of words or sentences due to midline problem

- Poor timing and sequencing in following class schedules and directions.

HANDWRITING

- Difficulty copying from the blackboard and from books

■ Fatigue easily when handwriting due to muscle tone

■ Pressure very light on writing utensil, often holding it at the distal tip; occasionally these children will do just the reverse and squeeze the pencil very hard in an effort to recruit more muscle power.

■ Poor or delayed hand dominance; may switch hands at midline when writing

■ May not stabilize paper when handwriting

STRATEGIES FOR THE DISORGANIZED CHILD CENTRAL VESTIBULAR/ PROPRIOCEPTIVE DYSFUNCTION

Strategies for the child with vestibular/ proprioceptive dysfunction involve providing appropriate movement opportunities, additional sensory cues/information, postural assistance, help to develop the use of two hands together, assistance for hand dominance development and crossing midline, strategies to improve sequencing and organization, and information to help in understanding the needs of student.

MOTOR PERFORMANCE/SELF CARE SKILLS

■ Provide opportunities for the child to move throughout the day, such as running errands, using different centers at which to work, and using movement in teaching. Provide a movement activity before settling down for homework.

■ Allow the child to sit on a gel or air filled cushion at his/her desk or table to provide sensory intake for movement and posture. This should be monitored carefully to be sure the movement is not too much for the child.

■ Allow the child to stand at the desk when appropriate. A marked square or circle made from masking tape on the floor gives a visual cue to help the child know the boundaries in which he/she can move without causing disruption to the class.

- A rocking chair is a very useful way to provide appropriate opportunities to move. Many teachers have such a chair in the reading corner. Many children like to rock while watching TV or reading.

- Proper positioning in a chair assists a child to sit at times when movement needs to be inhibited. This position is to have feet on the floor and lower extremity joints (hips and knees) at 90 degree angles, arms resting on the table top without causing the shoulders to elevate, and elbow joints at 90 degrees of flexion (bent).

- Encourage the child to keep desk and work spaces clear so that he/she can have enough space to work on crossing midline and to compensate as needed for when he/she cannot do so.

- Give verbal or tactile (touch) prompts to encourage use of both hands. For example, gently bring a neglected hand to the paper to help it stabilize the paper to print. A verbal cue might be to say, "Get both hands ready to catch this ball!"

- Provide opportunities to work in large spaces, such as the chalkboard and large coloring books. This encourages crossing midline.

- Use easy open cartons, and non-tip cups for lunch and snack.

Sensory Integration Strategies for Parents

■ Avoid difficult fasteners, use velcro or slip on sneakers when independence is needed.

FINE MOTOR/HANDWRITING

■ Grippers are usually helpful for these children to assist in grasp patterns and to maintain appropriate position on the pencil.

■ Short periods of writing at a time helps to prevent fatigue. Modifications may be needed as to quantity of writing required.

■ If chalkboard (far point) copying is difficult, provide a desk model so that the child can copy from closer range or near point copying.

■ Provide "wake-up" activities for hands before writing. These can be found in another section of this book.

■ Provide visual and auditory cues across midline. This might be to put a green for "go" line at the left side of the line and encourage your child to write all the way to the red line you drew at the end of the line.

■ Provide a visual model for letters on the desk. These adhesive strips are commercially available.

■ Use gum adhesive or tape to help stabilize paper for writing if the child cannot do so well enough with his non-dominant hand. Continue to encourage the use of both hands when writing or drawing – one hand to do the work and the other to hold the paper. Taping will just ease this while the child continues to learn to do so without help.

■ When a child has not yet established a hand dominance, be sure to hand pencils, utensils, or toys to him/her at the midline of the body so that a preference can become established by the child.

ACADEMICS/ORGANIZATION

■ Give frequent movement breaks throughout the day and during homework.

■ Use movement when studying or learning information. Try bean bag tosses and clapping rhythms to learn spelling, dancing to the words of a paragraph or the times tables, or singing the information to be memorized. Use your imagination.

■ Music is great to develop sequencing of information. It would be easier to learn your address and phone number if it had a song. Many children have learned the alphabet and some have learned all the names of the US presidents in order, by learning a song to that effect. Commercially available programs use music and songs to teach social studies, math, and science. Children with vestibular processing difficulties often benefit from these strategies.

CLASSROOM AND HOME SENSORIMOTOR INTEGRATION ACTIVITIES FOR THE CHILD WITH VESTIBULAR PROPRIOCEPTIVE PROCESSING DYSFUNCTION

These are everyday enjoyable activities that are based on sensory integration concepts and are helpful to enhance sensory processing.

- Movement opportunities could include jumping jacks, big arm swings, and jogging in place before doing an intense concentration task. These are short and intense and can be done quickly before the task. An abbreviated Simon Says also provides sequencing in a quick movement activity.

- Use scooters, bicycling, ice skating, roller skating, swimming, and playground visits to provide organized movement opportunities.

- "Wake- up" activities for the hands before writing could include the use of therapy putty or clay, squeeze balls and toys, and shaking Koosh balls.

- Provide activities that require the use of two hands. There are many activities for many age levels. Some examples are:

> lanyards, lacing, and sewing crafts
> manipulative put together toys or constructive
> building sets
> stringing beads

> playing with large balls, parachutes,
> rolling out clay with rolling pin
> stencils, templates
> ball games with a tool such as batting a ball,
>   tennis, T-ball, or golfing
> Etch-a Sketch

- Provide activities that require and assist in crossing the midline of the body such as erasing a large area on the chalkboard, finger painting, coloring large areas, two handed tasks such as swinging a baseball bat, and games such as Twister or Body Boggle.

- Stand back to back with a child or have two children stand back to back together. Using a playground ball or weighted ball pass the ball to each other by rotating the torso and using two hands on the ball at all times. This helps the children to cross the body midline by rotating around it.

- Sequencing games such as hopscotch, Cat's Cradle, hand clapping rhythm games.

A DAY IN THE LIFE OF VICKI: A CHILD WITH CENTRAL VESTIBULAR/PROPRIOCEPTIVE PROCESSING DYSFUNCTION (revisited)

Remember Vicki, the Kindergarten student with vestibular/proprioceptive dysfunction? Her parents and teachers put a few modifications into her day to help her progress in her skills.

Vicki now begins her day with lots of movement. She jumps on her small exercise trampoline and uses a hippity hop ball for a few minutes each morning. She still struggles with buttons but her mom bought her some pretty pullover dresses and shirts. She practices the buttons when she is not rushing to school. She has a large doll that she dresses each day after school. Sometimes her mom plays a silly game with Vicki in which they dress the child size chair in Vicki's room with Vicki's very own clothes. Vicki is remembering to hold the cereal bowl with her non-dominant hand as she sees her breakfast mat has a picture of two hands on the bowl.

At school, Vicki also has pictures to help her sequence the arrival routine. This helps her remember. She now sits on an air filled cushion to give her some movement input and keep her more alert. She never seems to slump in her chair any more. When she is using her crayons and pencils, Vicki remembers to do the "wake up" hand exercises her OT taught her. She gets both of her hands working together and does not fatigue as quickly as she used to. Sometimes, she still switches the paper instead of crossing the midline of her body. She plays lots of two-handed games and she is beginning to stick with one hand at a time.

Vicki does not seem to get as silly with movement in school anymore. Her mom provides a chewy food for both snack and lunch. Her teachers provide "heavy work" activity before gym and recess. Before recess she helps the teacher push the chairs into the desks and in gym she helps the teacher move some mats to the side of the room before the class. The gym teacher thought that adding some resistive activities to the curriculum seemed to help all the children, so routinely adds some wall pushups to each class.

Vicki still tends to have a high activity level. She is learning, with the help of her parents, OT, and teachers to identify when she is getting too active or silly and learning strategies to help her self calm. She is learning to do chair pushups, wall pushups, and hand- to- hand pushups. Her teacher has also learned to help Vicki identify the "warning signs" that she is getting too silly. At that point her teacher may ask Vicki to do an "errand" for her, or the teacher may give Vicki some firm pressure on the shoulders to provide a calming input. This is done inconspicuously, as the educator walks around the room to provide individual help to all the students. Vicki's OT has instructed the teacher how to provide this input in the right direction with the appropriate resistance for Vicki's body.

Sensory Integration Strategies for Parents

THE SENSITIVE CHILD

❖

SENSORY MODULATION DYSFUNCTION

THE SENSITIVE CHILD:

A DAY IN THE LIFE OF A CHILD WITH SENSORY MODULATION DYSFUNCTION

This is a fictional account of a very real problem. While Mike and his day do not truly exist, many children experience days like this all the time. You might recognize someone you know.

Mike is a 4-year-old child who has difficulty processing sensory information. He has a sensory modulation dysfunction. Mike cannot efficiently process information from the vestibular, auditory, tactile, or oral sensory systems. He attends a special education preschool classroom.

Mike's day begins with getting dressed, or should I say, fighting against being dressed by his father. He runs away as his dad tries valiantly to get Mike's pajamas off and his clothing on. He cries as Dad brushes his hair, and he won't even open his mouth to get his teeth brushed. He eats pancakes without syrup or butter for breakfast- the same breakfast he has eaten every day for the past year. He will only drink milk from the plastic cup with the monkey on it; heaven forbid if it is missing.

Mike goes to school on a school bus where his teachers help him get off the bus. He comes in crying, as he cannot tolerate the noise of the other children on the bus. His teachers take him to a quiet spot in the classroom so that he can take off his coat – slowly.

As the children gather for circle time, Mike cannot sit still and has trouble paying attention. He is constantly getting up from his seat. The other children are getting too close to him and he cries as if he has been hurt badly. He has, on occasion, hit children who bumped into him or leaned against him. He holds his hands over his ears as the children sing. The art and educational projects are a struggle for Mike. He has poor fine motor skills, as he never wants to touch anything – least of all glue or paint.

At snack time, Mike eats only yellow goldfish crackers and drinks from a juice box. He never eats any of the creative food projects presented by his teachers or shows interest in what the other children are eating.

At home, Mike prefers to watch videos or wander about his playroom, rarely playing with any toy for more than a few minutes. His father describes him as a whirlwind "who never seems to stop moving." He has a very difficult time getting to sleep, until he gets so overtired and "wound up," that he simply crashes wherever he happens to be. Sometimes, he does calm down with a warm bath and lots of cuddly blankets and some days his dad can actually get him into bed this way. Thank goodness he does sleep through the night.

SIGNS AND SYMPTOMS OF SENSORY MODULATION DYSFUNCTION

THE SENSITIVE CHILD

The Child with Sensory Modulation Dysfunction
Overview

There are several types of sensory modulation problems that impact on a child at home, in school, and at play. Children can present a *hyperesponsive* reaction and/or a *hyporesponsive* reaction to sensory intake.

A *hyperesponsive* reaction is an unusually strong or aversive response to sensations that would not typically be considered noxious. This is often called **sensory defensiveness**. Sensory avoidance is also seen.

A *hyporesponsive* reaction is one where the child seems to under react to sensory input, often needing more than average sensory input in order to react or seem to "feel" the input. These behaviors can take the form of a flat or unreactive appearance, but can also take the form of what is called **sensory seeking** behavior. The unreactive appearance can be a problem in registering or noticing the input. Sensory seeking behavior is seen when a child just can't seem to "get enough" sensory input and is constantly seeking out specific stimuli in the environment.

A child's reactions can often appear to swing from one end of the spectrum to the other (hyperresponsive to hyporesponsive), with little time spent in the midrange where organized behavior is seen. A most significant problem in sensory modulation dysfunction is these fluctuating reactions and behaviors that interfere with organized behavior. A child can be both sensory defensive to some sensory input and sensory seeking of other sensory stimuli. This can occur across sensory systems as well as within the same system. This is because sensory modulation dysfunction is about the regulation of the sensory "state" of a child, more than it is about individual sensory systems. Yet, we can discuss the behaviors in terms of individual sensory systems in order to learn and understand the presentations of sensory modulation dysfunction.

A child may present some of the sensory defensive behaviors and some of the sensory seeking behaviors that will be described. They may present sensory processing inefficiency in one sensory system, some sensory systems, or in all of them. Each child is unique. Also, sensory modulation problems often occur in conjunction with the other sensory integration deficits described in this book. Motor and self care skills may not develop as age appropriate due to an avoidance of these tasks, secondary to defensive reactions.

Some of the most common reactions/behaviors and how they affect a child are described. The following provides samples of the types of problems these children **may** experience in each area. Children may exhibit some of these but not necessarily all of them.

SIGNS AND SYMPTOMS OF VESTIBULAR/ PROPRIOCEPTIVE MODULATION DYSFUNCTION

Deficits in modulating the vestibular system can take the form of an overreaction, an underreaction, or a fluctuation between the two. They are most commonly related to a child's movement reactions.

Vestibular Defensive or Hyper-responsive Vestibular Behaviors

This child may be extremely fearful of movement due to an over reaction to vestibular input. The child with aversion to movement may even experience physical symptoms typical of excessive movement experiences with very little movement actually occurring.

- Unreasonable fear or physiological reaction to movement equipment in playground or home (increased heart rate, blood pressure, nausea, sweating)

- May get carsick on bus or other vehicles, increased dizziness

- Fearful of heights

- Stressed or fearful in physical education class or group activities

- Difficulty engaging in play activities with other children, due to fear of movement

■ Avoidance of movement; this may interfere with motor skill development such as climbing, balance reactions, and sports

■ Secondary interference with social/emotional areas due to above issues.

Vestibular Seeking
or Hypo-responsive Vestibular Behaviors
(craves movement)

This child does not interpret the vestibular intake efficiently and has an under reaction to movement. He/she, therefore, seeks more movement than the typical child. Another hyporesponsive reaction is to appear to be lethargic and/or sedentary.

■ Needs to move constantly, can't sit still, fidgets, rocks, may see head wagging or shaking

■ Difficulty paying attention, moves from task to task, constantly "on the go"

■ Easily over aroused or over stimulated with movement

■ Often lacks safety awareness or takes risks in movement activities

■ Appears lethargic and sedentary, may seem tired, muscle tone low

■ May tend to be sedentary, but once the child starts

moving may get too over stimulated, too quickly

Proprioceptive Seeking or Hypo-responsive Proprioceptive System

These behaviors suggest an inefficiency in processing proprioceptive information.

- Toe walking, foot slapping, forceful or abrupt movements, excessive jumping

- Pushes body or limbs hard against surfaces, may misjudge pressure applied or distance needed, hard pressure on pencil, may inadvertently break toys

- Wrapping legs up around seat or around own body (sits like a pretzel)

- Seeks out crashing, or chances to crash the body against surface (i.e. intentionally falls in play) May not be safety conscious

- Excessive biting or chewing on objects

- Poor motor planning or clumsiness, trips and falls a lot

- Poor awareness of body in space; can't seem to judge space of body

- May not grade touch, so seems to hit or overshoot when reaching or touching

- Hand flapping, finger flicking

SIGNS AND SYMPTOMS OF TACTILE SYSTEM MODULATION DYSFUNCTION

A child may present with a hyper or hypo responsive system or may vacillate between the two.

Tactile Defensiveness or Hyper-responsive Tactile Behaviors

Tactile defensiveness is an unusually aversive response to touch sensations that are not typically considered noxious. The child over reacts to touch sensations.

- Aversion to touch sensations, which are not typically considered noxious; can cause agitation or a feeling of being threatened

- Picks fights on line, fearful of moving children nearby, has difficulty staying in place on line, needs more personal space

- Fussy with clothing, may want to leave jacket on when entering room, dislikes changing clothes, prefers long sleeves and pants, dislikes tags in shirt

- Has difficulty changing the styles of clothing preferred, or the styles due to weather changes (from long to short sleeves, etc)

- Fussy regarding fabrics of clothing, towels, sheets

- Picky eater, fussy with food temperatures and textures

- Dislikes touching glue, finger paints, or any varied textures

- Distractibility is common, poor attention

- Dislikes grooming and hygiene activities such as haircuts, face washing, etc.

- Avoids hugs, infants tend to not be able to "mold" or be held

Tactile Seeking or Hypo-responsive Tactile Behaviors

This child does not register and process the tactile information he/she receives and seems to be unaware of many touch sensations. Others may exhibit "sensory seeking" tactile behaviors.

- Unaware of touch, may be unaware of his /her physical impact on other children, may not grade touch and seem to hit

- May bite or hit self

- May seem stoic or unaware of pain; never seems to be bothered by bumps or bruises; some children do not react to vaccinations or medical needles

- Sensory seeking may take the form of constantly seeking touch sensations by rubbing hands or body on objects or other people, pinching, or rubbing fingertips together

■ Sensory seeking children are often described as incessantly touching things or trouble "keeping hands to self"

SIGNS AND SYMPTOMS OF AUDITORY SYSTEM MODULATION DYSFUNCTION

Children can be sensitive or defensive to auditory input or sounds and noises. They can also seem to be unresponsive. Children can vacillate between the two.

Hyper Responsive Auditory Behaviors or Auditory Defensive Behavior

- Sensitive to, and distracted by sounds not noticed by others (for example- water running, fluorescent lights, fans humming, bugs, etc.)

- Poor attention

- Agitated by sounds, particularly fire drills or other loud noises, beepers and phones

- Distressed by sounds in physical education class, cafeteria, indoor swimming pools, restrooms

- Difficulty following auditory directions

- Difficulty in phonics, reading, spelling due to poor listening skills

- May have, or develop, auditory processing dysfunction concurrently

- Talks excessively or makes noises to avoid or dampen

sounds

- Biting and chewing also inhibit the intensity of sound heard by an individual; It is theorized that these strategies may sometimes be used by an auditory defensive child to inhibit sound.

Hyporesponsive Auditory Behavior

This is seen when a child is under-responsive to auditory input. The child seems unaware of sounds and noises. *Hearing loss must be ruled out first.*

- Does not respond when name is called

- Plays radio or TV louder than average

- Seeks out loud noises or may place ear close to sound sources

- Shows limitations in sounds produced

- May place ear on vibrating objects such as dishwasher, appliances, or dryer

SIGNS AND SYMPTOMS OF <u>VISUAL SYSTEM</u> MODULATION DYSFUNCTION

Children may experience a sensory defensive reaction or a sensory seeking reaction to visual sensory information. They may also experience a vacillation between the two.

Visual Defensive Behavior or Hyper-Responsive Visual Behavior

- Easily distracted visually

- Agitated by visual intake not normally noticed by others (ie. bright colors, fluorescent and bright lights, sunshine, jewelry, classroom decorations, etc.)

- Uncomfortable with the changing visual environment (children and objects moving unpredictably, objects moving towards them)

- Avoids eye contact, squints, hides eyes, shuts eyes

- Distressed when objects or environments are changed, (ie. new furniture, broken cookies, removal of old toys no longer played with)

Hyporesponsive Visual Behaviors

- Does not attend to visual stimuli, does not seem to focus

- Conversely may have fascination with edges, seams,

contrasting colors, patterns, seeks out bright colors

■ Difficulty negotiating floors with pattern or color changes (such as geometric tiles)

SIGNS AND SYMPTOMS OF ORAL/TACTILE SYSTEMS MODULATION DYSFUNCTION

The oral/tactile system is needed for taste and texture, to discriminate edibles from non-edibles, and to identify the source of nutrition (especially in infancy). It plays a significant role in organizing and developing a sense comfort and security. Inefficiency in this system may result in:

■ Feeding problems

■ Poor coordination of sucking, swallowing and breathing

■ Poor ability to switch from one nipple to another as an infant

■ Poor articulation, poor control of oral muscles

■ Picky eater, especially regarding textures

SIGNS AND SYMPTOMS OF OLFACTORY/GUSTATORY SYSTEMS MODULATION DYSFUNCTION

Olfactory/Gustatory Defensive Behavior (smell and taste)

- Distressed by smells in cafeteria, bathrooms

- Distressed by smell of pets, cooking odors, perfume, cleaning agents

- Picky eater, over responsive to unusual tastes or specific tastes

- Chews on erasers or mouth; chews non-edible objects

- Thumb sucking

- Poor oral motor development (drooling, loss of food, swallowing challenges, etc.)

Occasionally the gustatory system is **hypo-responsive**. This child seeks intense flavors and spices to "wake up their mouth." They often need the intensity to activate oral musculature as well.

The olfactory system is difficult to evaluate since it is a sensory system that has direct connections to our ancient roots for survival and protection. Strong emotional connections can be made with smells that involves more than sensory processing alone.

STRATEGIES TO HELP THE CHILD WITH SENSORY MODULATION DYSFUNCTION

Sensory modulation deficits are those deficits that interfere with the ability of the brain to regulate its own responses to sensory input. It may manifest in many different ways. The first set of strategies consists of general guidelines that are appropriate for all areas of sensory modulation deficits that are considered hyper responsive or defensive reactions. Following that are general guidelines for children who are hypo-responsive. Finally, there are suggestions more specific to each sensory area. *It is important to remember that not all of these strategies and guidelines are necessary, or appropriate, for all children with sensory processing dysfunction.*

GENERAL STRATEGIES FOR SENSORY DEFENSIVE BEHAVIOR

- Respect the child and what he/she is feeling. If a child feels that something is scary or hurtful, honor that feeling and do not belittle it. Comments such as "It doesn't hurt," or "That's not scary," are sometimes detrimental. It might be more beneficial to comment, "I know this is scary for you, but let's see how we can make you feel more comfortable with it," or, "Let's see if we can try it together!"

- Analyze the child's behavioral reactions to determine the possible cause of a strong reaction. Behavior is communication. Listen to it.

- Educate the student as to his/her specific processing patterns, and develop strategies to deal with the reactions and reduce stress. For example, a child who is tactile defensive might be told, "I know that it bothers you to touch this finger paint. Let's try to find some ways that you can paint without being bothered." Then problem solve together how the child can achieve the task with minimal or no stress. Explain to a child that he might like to stay last on line so other children will not bump into him.

- Educate people involved with your child, as appropriate, to understand the modulation problems of the child. Explain to a teacher that a tactile defensive child trying to pay attention in a classroom with many moving children, may be likened to trying to sit and pay attention in a classroom with a large wasp flying around your head. Both situations may require constant vigilance to the tactile threat rather than the cognitive lesson at the front of the room.

- Prepare your child for changes or incoming stimuli. For example, you might say, "I'm going to turn on the lights now," just before doing so. You might also say, "May I help you with your coat?" before touching the child or his clothing.

- Minimize the time your child spends in stressful situations, and allow the child some control over the situation to ease anxiety.

- Teach to a child's strengths. If a child shows auditory defensive behaviors, use a lot of visual cues and manipulatives in giving directions and teaching.

- Use oral organizing strategies as appropriate. See Oral Strategies section.
  > sucking foods are calming
  > crunching foods are alerting
  > chewing foods are organizing

- A calming center is a helpful addition to a younger classroom or at home. This is a sectioned off corner of the room where there are beanbag chairs, soft music with headphones, muted auditory and visual stimuli, and few children. The center provides a nurturing, calming, organizing place to go when a child needs it. This should clearly not be a punishment place but an *optional* learning place that is available to all children in the class, or at home, at various times. Guidelines for use must be established as per individual classroom/household needs.

■ Modify the environment as possible to minimize the stressors in the child's day.

GENERAL STRATEGIES FOR THE SENSORY HYPORESPONSIVE CHILD

CAUTION ABOUT THE SENSORY HYPORESPONSIVE CHILD

The child who appears to be HYPORESPONSIVE or UNDERRESPONSIVE to sensory input, **may** simply need to have increased sensory input and/or multi-sensory input to maximize learning and integration. *It is necessary to be cautious*, however, that the child who *appears* hyporesponsive may actually be extremely defensive. If this is the case, the child may be operating in a *shutdown mode* due to over arousal. In that event, high stimulation will just increase the problem. This is sometimes seen in children diagnosed with autism. It is very important to rule out any shutdown behaviors before providing any increased or high intensity sensory stimulation.

For children who are truly hyporesponsive the following general strategies may be helpful:

- Rule out shutdown. Children in shutdown will not respond favorably to increases in environmental stimuli, may shows signs of stress or anxiety with increases in environmental stimuli, or may withdraw more completely.

- Increase variety, novelty, unpredictability, frequency, and intensity of sensory input

- Make these changes gradually to be sure not to

overwhelm. It will make more sense if changes are made one at a time. For example, increase novelty but not intensity. Then, if needed, try them both together. In a tactile seeking child, this might take the form of first providing a variety of new tactile toys. If the child still seeks out input, then provide the variety of tactile toys with your interaction as well. This increases intensity with novelty.

- Combine multiple sensory systems. For example, provide a tactile toy with bright visual colors or music.

STRATEGIES TO HELP THE CHILD WITH SENSORY MODULATION DYSFUNCTION by SENSORY SYSTEM

This section is divided into the different sensory systems to help identify techniques for each area.

TACTILE SYSTEM

TACTILE DEFENSIVE/AVOIDANCE BEHAVIOR (HYPER-RESPONSIVE)

■ Avoid touching the head and face.

■ Avoid surprising or unpredictable touch.

■ Allow child extra personal body space. For example, keep school desks wide apart, place the child's desk in an area of less traffic, place the desk at the end of a row (not middle), and allow the child to go last on line. At home, do not seat children too close together at the dinner table or in the car, if possible. Try to keep "fidgety" children away from the tactile defensive child. Ask for restaurant tables that are not in a busy area of the room or ask for a booth.

■ Distinguish body space with a visual cue for the child and others in situations such as circle time or floor time. Carpet squares for children to sit on or masking tape squares on floor give a more defined space for younger children.

- Touch child firmly, not lightly. Avoid grabbing or poking. An open hand provides a firm touch that covers a wider space and is easier to tolerate.

- Allow the child time to adjust to clothing changes, such as taking jacket off when entering the classroom or coming home from the bus. Gradually introduce changes in clothing due to weather changes.

- Weighted wearables, such as vests or hats, provide a calming/organizing influence.

- Sensory stations or calming centers are a nice environmental modification that provide a release for tactile defensive children.

TACTILE SEEKING (HYPORESPONSIVE) **

- Provide opportunities to gain touch experiences throughout the day. This might take the form of covering textbooks or notebooks with textured fabric, using pens or pencils with varying textures, or keeping a texture key chain attached to pants or backpack/pocketbook. Some students do very well with a small stress ball type of object in their desk or pocket. These items must be quiet ones that are not visually stimulating or distractible in nature. They should not be used if the child becomes more interested in the object than the academic task at hand.

- Manipulative learning materials are very helpful

■ Combine tactile activities with proprioceptive activities

VESTIBULAR SYSTEM

VESTIBULAR DEFENSIVE/AVOIDANCE
HYPER-RESPONSIVE (gravitational insecurity and fear of movement)

■ Find playground tasks that the child can enjoy and feel comfortable doing. The goal is to find success. Bring in equipment if needed.

■ Encourage activities beginning with the least challenging, and moving on to more challenging. Least challenging activities are those that are lower to the ground, offer more control on the part of the child, and move more predictably.

■ Provide reassurance and encouragement.

■ When the child is engaging in movement activities such as climbing, hold firmly at the hips to help ground the child so that he/she feels safer; provide for enhanced deep pressure and proprioceptive intake by activity choice or consider a weighted wearable.

■ Don't force, but do encourage, movement activities. Allow the child to maintain control of movement as much as possible.

■ Provide chairs that support the child well and maintain feet on the floor.

VESTIBULAR SEEKING (HYPORESPONSIVE) ** (seeking /craving movement)

- Provide opportunities to move throughout the day. At school, this may be done by asking the child to run an errand or bring a book up to the front of the room. At home, schedule movement times between homework assignments and get outside to play whenever possible. Trips to the playground, swimming, roller skating, or bicycle riding are great movement opportunities.

- Provide "heavy work" opportunities. These are activities that cause the muscles and joints to work hard or against some resistance. A weighted vest, or a sandbag on the lap, provides additional sensory information.

- Schedule highly concentrative work periods after a period of movement such as physical education class or recess. Do a short movement activity before homework.

- Use short sessions of work interspersed with a *short* movement activity (ten jumping jacks, or a few tumblesaults). Some children do well with a timer to measure their work period.

- Avoid using recess as a time to make up work or for a punishment. This child needs to move, and missing recess will just accentuate the problem.

- Provide for calming centers or screened off work areas that all children may use to help increase concentration.

- Provide oral motor calming/organizing strategies. (see

oral strategies section).

- Use movement in teaching. The use of moving stations or standing at chairs is helpful. Have children use movement when learning a concept. This may be moving to a multiplication song or moving from standing to sitting to illustrate a concept.

AUDITORY SYSTEM

AUDITORY DEFENSIVE/AVOIDANCE
OR HYPERRESPONSIVE

- Try using headphones with calming music during noisy experiences, such as the bus.

- Seat the child near the doorway in the cafeteria or in an area of less traffic.

- Educate cafeteria staff and arrange opportunities for the child to "escape" the noise by helping out in a nearby area or arranging for early exit to recess.

- Try to limit time in noisy environments.

- Provide pleasing rhythmical and predictable music or sounds.

- Provide noise reduction/canceling headphones for select times and activities. Use judiciously.

- Allow for specified periods of time called "quiet time" for reading, homework, or relaxation.

- Speak softly and use a gentle tone of voice

- Help to develop auditory discrimination such as identifying common sounds, or on a higher level, identifying sounds of notes

- Provide calming input while in noisy environments (chewing gum, food, or appropriate object, providing deep pressure, etc.)

- Ask for a booth in restaurants. This helps inhibit background noise.

AUDITORY SEEKING OR HYPORESPONSIVE **

- Rule out hearing loss

- Investigate whether this is also an auditory processing or discrimination problem

- Vary the loudness of music and speaking activities

- Use the other senses to augment the auditory system – for example, demonstrate directions as well as giving them verbally.

- Many of the auditory processing strategies also help with this child. (See auditory processing section).

VISUAL SYSTEM

VISUAL DEFENSIVE/AVOIDANCE
HYPERRESPONSIVE

- Modify lighting where possible so that it is not overly bright. Avoid fluorescent lights. Some children prefer full spectrum natural light bulbs over the incandescent lights.

- Arrange section of the classroom, bedroom, or home areas that are less visually stimulating for concentrated work.

- Keep desks neat. Avoid clutter or too many knick-knacks.

- Arrange written handouts so that they are not excessively "busy" or contrasting.

- Use the cool color schemes (blues and greens) where possible.

- Allow the child to wear a hat or sunglasses in the bright sunshine. Don't seat the child in the sunshine when doing table or desk work.

- Shield parts of the paper from vision while working on one area. For example, only uncover one Math problem at a time.

VISUAL HYPORESPONSIVE **

- Use bright colors

- Use sharp contrasts.

- Add visual interest by adding detail to handouts or educational materials

OLFACTORY SYSTEM

OLFACTORY DEFENSIVE/AVOIDANCE OR HYPERRESPONSIVE

- Remember that all odors tend to be alerting.

- Arrange cafeteria setting as described in auditory defensiveness.

- Identify scents that are associated with pleasurable events or that the child finds comforting. Vanilla, lavender, and rose are generally felt to be calming scents while citrus, cinnamon, and mint, tend to be regarded as more invigorating scents. Check with aromatherapy experts for more information.

- Be aware of the child's reactions to cleaning agents used in the home, classroom, and bathrooms, and modify them as possible. Laundry products can also leave a strong scent. Investigate scent free cleaners.

- Avoid scented candles or perfumes that are unpleasant to the child.

OLFACTORY SEEKING **

- Some children seem to need to smell everything. This may be related to the need to gain more information through a sensory channel with which they are more comfortable, or which is more efficient for them. Providing pleasing smells may be helpful, but it is probably more helpful to improve the other sensory systems for gaining information.

- Some children may look for familiar odors to calm themselves. Help your child find additional calming strategies as well.

- Some children may seek out alerting scents to "wake up" the sensory system. Find additional and alternative alerting strategies.

- Try to analyze the child's olfactory preferences and how they impact on his/her behavior.

A DAY IN THE LIFE OF MIKE: A CHILD WITH SENSORY MODULATION DYSFUNCTION
(revisited)

Remember Mike, the four year old boy who has sensory modulation deficits and attends a special education preschool? His parents and teachers have put a few modifications into his day to make him more comfortable and consequently more cooperative throughout his day.

Mike hops out of bed in the morning and still hates getting dressed. His dad makes sure that he has his clean underwear on already from his bath the night before so that he has less to change in the morning. He has set up a small tent in his room with a sleeping bag in it. This minimizes the visual and tactile stimuli and provides a claming place for Mike. Sometimes he stays in the sleeping bag to change his clothes, and other days he can just change in the tent alone. His dad changes Mike's shirt first, then his pants. He makes sure that his son has a lot of his body covered at one time. Dad lets Mike brush his hair himself (some days it looks better than others), but he is learning that brushing hair is not so bad. Before he brushes his teeth, Mike chews on a chewy tube that his parents ordered from a catalog and dad helps him press firmly with his hands on his cheeks and face. He also uses a timer to let Mike know when he can stop brushing. Mike still eats a limited diet, but his dad is providing changes little by little. Some mornings he will change the brand of pancakes; some mornings he will give him milk in a different glass. Occasionally, Mike will get a different drink in the same cup. His father also offers Mike foods he likes in *combination with* new challenging foods. For example, he might offer his usual pancakes with a tiny bit of jelly on it. Mike is expected just to try the new item until he learns to try more and more.

At school, Mike's teachers have continued to provide him with opportunities to be in a quiet environment. They have a small area with beanbag chairs, limited visual stimulation, and headphones with specially selected music (modulation CDs or calming relaxation CDs). In circle time, he wears a weighted vest and is allowed to hold a small squeeze toy. The children have marked spots where they sit; sometimes they sit in the small chairs. Art projects are presented with gentle encouragement and are never forced. Mike is praised when he touches the challenging textures. He is allowed to touch with just one finger if necessary, and there is a wet paper towel by his side to encourage him to take that chance. Mike is also receiving OT at school.

At home, mom and dad have provided bedtime routines for him, which include a warm bath, followed by a *firm* towel rub. He then has warmed lotion applied to his legs, arms, and back with a very firm touch. His mom puts a lavender scent in the tub. There are extra towels and rugs in the bathroom to help inhibit the echoes and sounds, and the vent is not turned on. After bathing, Mike is wrapped in heavy blankets for a bedtime story that is relatively short. He also has extra pillows placed by the sides of his bed for more tactile input that is calming. Sometimes his mom places the weighted blanket over him as well. He listens to specifically treated music for sleeping, and he now falls to sleep much easier than ever before.

Mike continues to struggle with modulating his

sensory systems, and some days his parents, teachers, and OT are more successful in helping him than on other days. Little by little, they hope to decrease the amount of supports and modifications he needs. These will gradually be reduced. Mike will eventually be taught the strategies he needs to use to organize himself in order to attend and participate in school and home activities. His parents will look to find community activities that provide him with the proper amount of sensory input that he needs, so as to eventually discontinue his OT sessions.

PRACTICAL TASK STRATEGIES FOR THE SENSORY DEFENSIVE CHILD

It is the sensory defensive children who struggle just to tolerate the multitude of sensations that bombard their nervous systems constantly. These are the children who have such a difficult time tolerating haircuts, hygiene and grooming tasks, dressing, and just about every routine event. These strategies are for them. Try using one or all of these strategies, if necessary, to help your child tolerate these routine, but stressful, tasks. Try to use as few strategies as possible. Remember, your goal is to use fewer and fewer of them over time.

HAIRCUTS AND HAIR COMBING

Haircuts and hair combing do not have to be a "hair-raising" experience. Preparation, education, and grading are the keys.

HAIRCUTS:
- Play haircut games on dolls before each visit. You can use the commercially available modeling dough haircut kits, buy an inexpensive doll with hair and cut that, or pretend to cut with imaginary or plastic non cutting scissors on the doll. Paper doll haircuts are also good.

- Pretend to cut your child's hair with your fingers (no pulling, just whisk through slowly) but use pressure on the scalp. The next step is to play haircut with a gentle pull and release when you pretend "cut" with your fingers. Remember that your touch needs to be firm and not light or tentative. Let your child pretend cut your hair as well. You can play "buzz cuts" and/or trimmer using vibrating toys to simulate sound and sensation on head/neck area, but be careful that the vibration is not too strong, especially around the head.

- When haircut time is near, you might want to cut a few inconspicuous snips in your child's hair and let the clippings fall. Maybe your child can feel the small clippings and explore them.

- Massage your child's scalp whenever possible. *Use deep pressure*. Do this before combing hair each day as well. Use the pulling motion on the hair described above.

■ Visit the hairdresser to watch other people get haircuts. Be excited and positive. Find a child friendly hairdresser (ask other parents or therapists). Look how much fun it is!! Talk about what is happening. Ask the hairdresser if your child can sit in the chair a few minutes. Maybe the hairdresser can even move the chair up and down for the child.

■ Practice putting on the cape. Use a pretend cape at home or have a trial at the hairdresser. Make sure the cape is not tight around the child's neck.

■ Whenever possible, use a cape because it keeps the itchy hair clippings away from the body. If not possible – get a haircut anyway. Use a large soft T-shirt as a cape, or bring a change of clothes for after haircut if the T-shirt doesn't work. Baby powder after a haircut helps to smooth away the itchy hair clippings.

■ A shampoo at the hairdresser is often difficult. Most hairdressers will let you come with the hair washed at home.

■ The spray bottle is hard to take because it is unpredictable, often cold, and is a light touch. Try to avoid the water spray near the face – use your hands to block the water if possible, and assure your child that the water will not spray the face (and make sure it doesn't if you say so!). Play with a spray bottle at home in the bathtub or kitchen. Let the child spray and explore. Start spraying arms and legs before you try to spray the head. In the winter you can spray the snow with water colored with food coloring. Children can also spray tinted water on paper or coffee filters in the kitchen. Food coloring does stain so be careful of your house and clothing.

■ Remember to be positive and prepare your child in a fun and playful way. Do not present negative or fearful ideas.

HAIR COMBING/BRUSHING:

Allow your child to do as much combing for themselves as they can. Giving the child control is a critical piece to increase tolerance. You can also let your child hold the brush with you. Remember to praise the effort and not to worry if the style is not always perfect.

■ Use deep pressure massage prior to combing, and use a firm touch when combing.

■ Hold the ends of the longer hair to prevent too much pulling. Brush or comb from the bottom first.

■ Limit the time spent brushing. A few knots left in the hair is not critical. Let your child have breaks from brushing if needed.

■ Consider the hairbrush bristles – some are softer, some are closer together, some cause more static. The choice is dictated by thickness of hair, curl of hair, and child preference. Generally, plastic wider bristles cause less static and go through hair quicker, but they can sometimes be too hard on the scalp. Look for the little rounded edges on bristles. If possible, have several choices for a child to try, to see what feels more comfortable. Make it a fun experiment.

■ Maintain brushes in good condition to maximize efficiency and prevent unnecessary harshness. The little knobs on the ends of some plastic bristles will often fall off, making the bristles sharp and uncomfortable. Replace them right away.

■ Consider using spray-in detanglers but hold the spray bottle away from the face. Try cupping your hand towards the nozzle and aiming any stray sprays away from the face. Cream rinses and conditioners are also helpful

■ Keep the hairstyle short. Minimize use of clips and rubber bands. Be sure to use the coated hair rubber bands if you need them.

TRIMMING/CLIPPING NAILS

So many children have difficulty tolerating nail trimming, that many parents have resorted to trimming them while the child is sleeping. These strategies are designed to make the move to doing it while your child is awake!

- Fingernail clipping is usually more tolerated than toenail clipping so start with fingernails.

- Play nail trimming games with pretend clippers or scissors. Press a dull object firmly on your child's nails and pretend to "clip."

- Allow your child to play the same game on their own nails as well as on yours.

- With real clippers, show your child how the clippers work on a piece of paper.

- Use Emory boards to firmly file on nails.

- Many girls are motivated to play nail polish. This helps increase tolerance to handling the nails in a playful and motivating manner.

- When actually trimming the nails, hold toes/fingers firmly all together in one grip with space for you to clip the nails. Do not move the individual toes/fingers around but keep them comfortably tucked in your hand.

- Use firm pressure at all times – avoid excessive movement and use a firm grip.

- Make sure that the clippers or nail scissors you use are sharp and efficient so that the job is done quickly.

- Don't feel that you have to do all the nails the same day. You may need to just do one or two at first and gradually build up to all 10 or 20.

CLOTHING/DRESSING

- Honor your child's preferences for clothing choices when possible. Try to be flexible as to what is "appropriate" by our standards.

- Some children will need the socks inside out, tags cut off, softer pants without zippers or buttons, etc. Waistlines are often difficult to manage. Cotton is often the more easily tolerated fabric. Many clothes are now made with printed labels instead of tag labels. These are excellent.

- Some children have trouble with heavy coats or thick and fluffy down feather coats. They may do better with layers rather than one heavy coat. The newer lightweight fabrics often work well. Soft thermal clothing adds warmth without thickness.

- Many children with modulation and regulation difficulties tend to stay warmer than average. Know your child and dress them for the weather for THEM not US.

- Many children have difficulty feeling the change of air on their bodies as they change clothing. Some do well changing clothing under the covers or in sleeping bags.

- Try changing only one piece of clothing at a time, replacing that piece, then moving to the next item.

- Provide something to suck on, gum to chew, calming music, or visual distraction to calm during dressing.

- When diapering, consider the temperature changes – especially using wipes. Try warmer temperatures if possible. Wipe warmers are commercially available. Place a firm comforting hand to the baby's chest when the diaper is off to the calm and comfort.

- Many children have difficulty tolerating the change of clothes appropriate to the season. Layers work well as the temperatures change. Pants that have zippers on the legs to change from shorts to long pants, and the reverse, help children tolerate the changes.

- Shoelaces may need to be tighter or looser than what we determine to be "appropriate." Make sure they are safe and honor those preferences. Many children prefer slip on shoes.

- Many children can tolerate clothing better if provided with a firm hug or deep pressure before dressing.

- Some children like the firm pressure felt when wearing a spandex shirt or shorts under the clothing. Bike shorts work well for this. A girl's one-piece bathing suit or leotard is comforting, but remember that these can make toileting a nightmare. You can try to cut the bottom open to make the suit or leotard function like a long shirt. Commercially available pressure clothing is available, but should be used under the guidance of your occupational therapist.

- Try to develop a dressing routine. Predictability is calming and organizing. Picking out clothing for the next day the night before is sometimes helpful. Be aware, however, that this is not foolproof, and changes may be requested by your child the next morning. If choosing becomes a battle, allow a choice of two items and do not allow rummaging through piles of clothing or multiple changing of outfits.

- Too much dressing to do in the morning is often stressful for parents and children alike. Plan for some of the clothing items to be donned the night before. For example, clean underwear at night rather than the morning might minimize the amount of morning dressing.

- Hats and mittens are often intolerable. Let your child play with these items before asking for them to be worn. Hats that tie under the neck are harder to tolerate than those that do not. Many children can tolerate hoods or baseball caps better than tied or fitted hats. Mittens are usually easier to tolerate than gloves. The act of putting on gloves (fitting each individual finger in the sleeve) is usually difficult to tolerate. If your child is one who likes pressure clothing, fitted knit hats may be preferred.

- Female teenagers may need to wear cotton sport bras or well fitted bras without excessive seams, underwires, or metal clasps on shoulders.

BATHING

Many children love the bath, but some find it a sensory defensive experience. Some enjoy it while they are in it, but become overly alert from the multiple stimuli they experience. The bath provides multiple sensory stimuli. The touch of the water and soap, hair washing, sounds from echoes, smells of soap, visual stimuli of splashing and soap bubbles, and towel drying all contribute to an intense sensory experience. Yet, the warm water and deep pressure from the water can also be very calming and relaxing. Know your child to make the decisions that would be most beneficial.

- Consider the time of day that the bath experience would be most beneficial. Calming baths before bedtime make it part of a good routine for some children. If bath time is very alerting, plan the bath when you have time to do some calming strategies following the bath.

- Routines are helpful to organize and calm. Do not, however, encourage strict non-deviating routines as that can become just as obstructive. Many children with sensory modulation deficits look for strict routines in hygiene to provide control of the situation. These can be maladaptive of they become too rigid.

- Deeper water provides more deep pressure than just a small amount of water in the tub. Deep pressure tends to be more calming.

- Honor water temperature requests within reason.

- Consider room temperature. Warm is generally calming, colder is generally alerting.

- Consider scents used. Some children need odorless materials; some may respond to calming vanilla or lavender, or an energizing orange.

- Use of soap – bar soap, liquid soap, suds, all have a different impact. Suds tend to be more alerting, liquid soap is usually more calming (can be rubbed firmly). Bar soap presents more control and is therefore less alerting, as long as it doesn't easily slip out of the hands. Try to use a bar soap that has a simple shape for holding onto.

- Sounds in the bathroom are often echoed or distressing. Try to provide extra mats or carpeting or drape towels where possible to dampen the echo and mute the sound vibrations. This is also true when flushing the toilet. The sound often frightens children with auditory problems. Sometimes opening the door is helpful to balance out the echoes.

- Allow child to chew gum for a calming input during bathing.

- Limit the amount of water toys in the tub. The water toys that are provided should be smooth and not overly textured, or offer soothing sounds or visual input. Squeezing toys and sponges are good for calming. Avoid very busy or alerting toys.

- Some children tolerate bathing better if allowed to wear a bathing suit in the tub until he/she gets more used to it

HAIR WASHING IN THE BATH:

Most children have their hair washed in the bathtub. Consider these suggestions for in or out of the tub. Does your child respond better if you wash the hair in the tub or outside in the sink?

- Shampoos that have conditioner and shampoo together eliminate a step.

- Rub firmly but not harshly-avoid light touch. Avoid poking touch.

- Use as little shampoo as possible to make rinsing that much faster and to eliminate an overabundance of suds.

- Have your child help pour the water to rinse. Control of the situation helps increase comfort level.

- Rinsing with a plastic handled spout pitcher helps control dripping. Showers that have moveable or hand held showerheads also provide for more control of the water.

- Have your child "rinse" some of the soap out by putting their head into the tub water themselves. Then you have less to rinse with the poured water.

- Have a washcloth or small hand towel handy to dry eyes and ears. Some children like a visor to keep water from eyes. Some children like earplugs to alleviate the feeling of water on or in the ear.

- Rinse a little at time.

- Give breaks as needed. Wash hair, rinse a little, play a little, rinse a little more, etc. *Occasionally*, it is better, however, to get it all over at once if possible.

DENTIST VISITS

Dental visits are a very stressful activity for many people with sensory processing dysfunction. Most of us probably find work inside our mouths by a dentist to be somewhat invasive. Find a dentist who is sensitive to these needs and who will work with you and your child. If possible, interview the dentist first so you can determine if he/she is right for you and your child.

■ Prepare by talking to your child about the dentist in a positive way. There are many books about going to the dentist that explain the process. Talk to your dentist prior to visit to discuss your child's special needs. Find a dentist who understands and will work with you.

■ Play dentist games. There are many commercially available games that use teeth and mouths for younger children. You can also use a mirror to look at your mouth and your child's mouth. Let your child look inside your mouth and you look inside your child's mouth. You can touch his/her teeth to count them. Be very careful not to put your finger too far back into the mouth or you will stimulate a gag reflex.

■ There are many strategies to help decrease sensory defensive behavior around and in the mouth. These are best directed by an occupational therapist or speech therapist. In general, however, touching the face with deep pressure is usually more tolerable than light touch. Touching the face and lips needs to be tolerated before touching inside the mouth. Many children can tolerate dental work better if preparatory deep pressure and proprioceptive activities are provided before the visit.

- The use of safety gloves, whether latex or not, still creates a distinct smell, feel, and taste. Try to find out the type of gloves the dentist will use and ask for a pair to practice with – for taste, smell, and feel. Let your child wear them and put his own fingers into his mouth. Then see if he can let you try. Remember not to move far back into the mouth or you will create a gag.

- Try to give your child an opportunity to sit in the dental chair on a separate visit before the work is to be done. Have the dentist move it up and back (especially back as that is more threatening). Ask the dentist to show your child one or two tools that are not threatening. Some dentists will let the child feel the "toothbrush" on the back of the hand to see how it moves and feels.

- Ask the dentist to divide the work to be done into gradual SHORT visits. This will only be necessary for extensive work. Most children need a simple and quick cleaning.

- The lead apron used for x-rays is very heavy and provides calming deep pressure input. Your child may be calmed by wearing it for the entire visit. Some children may use weighted vests or weighted lap objects as well. These are better if the child is already using them and they are already familiar.

- Consider background noises and music. Is your child hearing the drill from another room? Is the music calming for your child? Try headphones with preferred music or sound dampening headphones.

■ Ask the dentist to make sure the light is not shining too much into your child's eyes. If possible, turning off the light may be helpful. Some children have actually worn sunglasses to minimize the light impact. What does the child see when the chair is tilted? A familiar or calming picture or object might be helpful.

■ Give your child some control. A hand signal that the child can use when he/she needs a brief respite goes a long way to reassuring, calming, and encouraging trust in the dentist.

TOOTHBRUSHING

- Allow your child to do as much as possible, independently. If needed, have your child place a hand over yours to help. Control of the situation is helpful for the child.

- Limit time spent brushing. Allow child to take a brief stop if needed. Use a timer for a visual cue to help your child know when brushing is done.

- Some children respond to deep finger massage on gums and teeth prior to brushing. This can be done by parent or child. Be sure not to stimulate a gag reflex by moving too far back into the mouth, on the roof of the mouth, or tongue.

- Try letting your child "brush" his teeth with his finger and toothpaste, initially. There is a new commercially available product that is placed on the finger to brush the teeth.

- Some children respond well to electric toothbrushes.

- Limit the amount of toothpaste used.

- Provide a washcloth for your child to clean the mouth of any drips.

- Consider different tastes and textures of toothpaste. There are many varieties on the market that can be explored. Mint and cinnamon flavors tend to be alerting.

- Consider the type of toothbrush used. Shorter ones are generally easier for your child to control and are less intimidating. Make sure your child has enough control to avoid pushing the brush too far into the mouth. Bristle hardness makes a big difference. Most children do better with softer bristles.

MAKING TRANSITIONS

Transitions from place to place, activity to activity, or from the state of alertness to a new state of alertness are often difficult for children with sensory processing problems. Some suggestions are as follows.

PLACE TO PLACE or ACTIVITY TO ACTIVITY:

- Give a 2 or 5 minute warning for the change depending on the age of the child and the level of difficulty the child experiences with change.

- Some children do well with a visual timer to prepare for change- hourglass egg timers for children who do not understand numbers, or number timer for older children. Make sure the ring is not too startling for auditory defensive children. There are commercially available timers that are designed as a clock face with a changing red "slice of pie" to demonstrate the passage of time.

- Another visual aid could be to slowly fill a jar with marbles as the task continues, placing one marble every predetermined passage of time. Once the jar is filled, it is time to change the activity. A similar concept is to little by little move an object towards a target. For example, every few minutes, the car draws closer to the garage. Once the car is in the garage, the activity is finished.

- Provide a "transition activity." The goal is to make the transition itself a new and enjoyable activity. For example, "Let's march to the next room," or "who can sing a song while we clean up this toy?" Provide an "important job" to do for the transition. For example, "please help me carry this item to the next place or activity." For older children, the transition activity might be more time oriented such as providing a 5 minute transition break activity. This activity could be a quick snack or a chance to look briefly at a preferred book or magazine. Adhere strictly to the time that is predetermined.

- Music is an excellent facilitator. Sing a transition song that has a slow but clear beat. For example, the old Mickey Mouse Club song "Now It's Time to Say Goodbye," or "Good Night Ladies," or one of the "famous" clean up songs. Make up your own words to any song that tells what you are about to do. For older children, start playing a calming piece of music that will signal the end of the activity when the music ends. Continue to play the calming music while transitioning if possible. Older children can also hum a soothing rhythm for transitions.

- Be enthusiastic about the change. Tell your child what the next "exciting event" will be. "Let's go see Daddy!" "It's time for…."

- Be supportive that the child may be disappointed. You might want to acknowledge that fact with a short simple sentence but do not linger on it. You may want to say, "I know that you are sad (disappointed) to stop now, but we are going to…. Or we have to…"

- Be consistent. Do not irregularly give in to "one more

time" or 5 more minutes.

■ Provide a consistent and clear set of expectations for behavior.

CHANGING STATES OF ALERTNESS OR ACTIVITY:

Most of us need time to adjust from a time of alerted excitement to a calm state. This change is very hard for children with sensory processing problems. This difficulty often occurs at nap or bed time or following a very exciting activity.

■ Provide calming activities using sensory strategies. Calming activities are slow, rhythmic, and predictable sensory input using movement, touch, sound (music), and vision. Neutral warmth is also calming (bath, blankets, cuddles).

■ Provide oral calming strategies such as sucking, drinking, or chewing.

■ Use a soft well modulated tone of voice.

■ Use songs as described above.

■ Be consistent. Provide routines.

■ Provide a non-stimulating visual environment or have your child move out of the busy environment. If this is not possible, have him look towards a visually calmer area of the room.

■ Be aware of other activities in the same room or area- are they causing increase in excitement?

PARTIES/ PUBLIC PLACES/ SCHOOL BUS

Going to new places or tolerating noisy or busy environments can be extremely challenging for children with sensory modulation dysfunction as well as their parents. Not only do parents have to deal with their child's responses and their own feelings, but they are often confronted by a barrage of well intentioned advice from others. Many parents also have to deal with the hurt feelings from other adults who may not have the understanding of the challenges the family is facing.

- Talk with your child about upcoming events and places to visit in a positive but brief way. Too much discussion will lead to anxiety. Some children need more time in advance, some do better with notice that is not so far in advance. Some children develop a great deal of anxiety if events are discussed too far in advance because they spend too much time thinking about the unknown upcoming event. No one likes to worry about an unknown event for very long. You know your child and can plan the timing of the conversation.

- Have trial runs if possible. A bus ride, a visit to school, or a visit to the party location, can help alleviate many fears.

- Go a little bit early to parties so people are added gradually and your child does not walk into a crowded room.

- Try to find quiet spots at a party or social outing for brief respite when you see signs of stress. The front seat of a bus might be easier to handle than the middle or back.

Some children actually prefer the *back* of bus, however, because they can see what is going on, and it is more predictable – less alarming.

■ If attending a quiet event, such as religious services or performance, provide as much movement as possible before the event to help your child sit still. Provide movement breaks to the rest rooms or other appropriate areas.

■ Bring a sensory strategy object, special toy, or oral food item for calming. For the bus provide a book to read or music headphones. Some children do well with a weighted vest for bus rides or short visiting events. For religious services or quiet events, try chair push ups, pressing hands together forcefully, or deep pressure on the shoulders.

■ In the grocery store, have your child help push the heavy cart, or use one of the child carts, often provided, loaded with a few cans for weight. You can also have your child help you carry some "heavy" items.

■ Don't force your child to say hello and kiss everyone at social events. A wave might be a good strategy. Ask family and friends to respect what is needed by your child right now.

■ Give your child his/her own time to warm up to a social event or activity. Gentle encouragement and patience goes a lot further than force.

■ Limit time in the stressful setting. For example, initially, try the bus ride *home only*. Have your child board the bus home LAST. Leave the party a bit early if necessary. Sometimes, however, it is at the end of the party when your child is now finally warming up!

■ Try to go to shopping or crowded events at a less crowded time.

■ A comforting friend on the bus or at an event is often helpful.

■ Be positive and encouraging and know that you will be successful. Don't expect changes to occur overnight. Little by little you will see your child become more engaged and content in these situations. As they become more comfortable you can decrease the assistance and/or increase the challenges.

SLEEPING

Sleeping is a complex matter for many children with sensory integration deficits. The full topic of sleep and sleep disorders is well beyond the scope of this book and this author's expertise. However, there are some suggestions for helping children get to sleep, which may prove useful. It is important to note, however, that sleeping and getting to sleep is far more than a sensory integration issue and needs to be looked at from a behavioral, habitual, and physiological aspect. Medical issues, such as sleep apnea and even enlarged tonsils and adenoids can influence sleep and its patterns. **It is strongly recommended that parents consult their pediatrician if sleep concerns are present.**

- Most children do well with bedtime routines (not strict rituals) that provide predictability and are calming. The activities should be done in the same order.

- Listening to special sleep CDs or classical music is helpful. Continuous play CD players are nice because many children wake up to the click of the stop of the player.

- Weighted blankets or many layered blankets provide deep pressure that is calming and relaxing. Be sure that your child can move safely under these blankets.

- Warmth is more calming than cold, but some children can become fussy if it is *too hot*.

- Repetitive sounds are more calming for sleep than

irregular sounds. Listen for any irregular background noises that my be alerting your child.

■ A warm bath, followed by a firm towel rub, tends to calm children for sleep.

■ Try to provide a rigorous exercise approximately 4- 6 hours before bedtime.

■ Avoid rigorous activities right before bed.

■ Warm milk and turkey do have a natural chemical, called tryptophan, which is believed to induce sleep.

■ Keep bedrooms visually calming and non-stimulating. For example, use soft colors, minimize clutter, and avoid disrupting light either from indoor or outdoor lighting.

■ Avoid the use of the bedroom for stimulating activities.

■ Avoid stressful activities before bedtime.

EATING

Many children with sensory integration dysfunction are, what is called, "picky eaters." This is an extensive topic that truly requires more attention than can be addressed in the scope of this book. It is suggested that you consult with a professional who specializes in this area. These are general guidelines or strategies to try.

■ Consider which utensils are being used. Do they fit into the child's mouth properly? Are there any rough edges? Are they comfortable for your child?

■ Textures of food are often culprits in picky eating. Look for patterns in your child's food choices. Are they avoiding certain textures such as smooth, crunchy, sticky, chewy, or multi-textured?

■ Appearance of food can be problematic for some children. Look for patterns that seem visual – are they upset by "broken" cookies or the color of food? Try to vary the visual presentation of food with cheerfulness and confidence.

■ Introduce new foods in small doses with small changes.

■ Do not make eating new foods a power struggle or a forced situation. Try to make it a voluntary and enjoyable experience by your presentation and modeling.

■ Model your own good eating habits of trying new foods.

- Make food "fun" by its appearance and presentation. For example, make pancakes or sandwiches with a funny face or have a picnic on the kitchen floor or backyard.

- Many children (especially younger ones) like dipping foods, such as carrots, into dressing

- Allow your child to just try a *small amount of new food* – even a lick, if necessary- and then throw out the food. Some children can only tolerate putting a new food to their lips for a second. Take time, and give time.

- Pair foods that they do not like with foods that they do. For example, pair a non- preferred carrot with a dip into well loved peanut butter.

- Make small variations in food to increase tolerance to variety – change brands, packaging, style of preparation, and even the bowls/cups the food is served in. For example, use sliced cheddar instead of American cheese or change the brand of bread. Change the colors and/or shapes of cups and bowls.

- Offer variety at each meal, but you may not want it all on the same plate at the same time. You may need different plates, or to present two to three foods at a time. Try not to present so much variety at one time that it is visually overwhelming.

- Give the child some control and say as to what they might be willing to try

- Be positive and encouraging even though, at times, it

may become very frustrating. Praise each accomplishment, no matter how small.

- Initially, try to introduce new foods that are *similar* to what they already like. For example, if yogurt is preferred, introduce smooth pudding and then tapioca pudding. If peanut butter and jelly on white bread is preferred, introduce peanut butter with apple butter or jelly with cream cheese. Or, you can change the white bread to a light whole wheat bread. Gradual changes are easier to make.

- Prepare the mouth to eat before eating. This may take the form of firm pressure to lips and cheeks with hands or washcloth. Or you can play with a lollipop or toothbrush in the mouth. Rub the insides of the cheeks, gums, teeth, and tongue with firm pressure.

- Use activities from the Sensory Oral Motor Section of this book

- Some children and families do better if they try the new food apart from the regular meal time initially, and gradually add that new food to mealtime

- Some children are more willing to try a new food when they are hungry (but not so extremely hungry that they are cranky). Most will not try a new food when they are already satisfied.

- Consider nutrition. Give supplements if necessary. Poor or limited eating tends to decrease appetites for volume and quality food.

- Consider dental health. Dental problems can interfere with eating and poor eating can influence dental health. See Dentist Visits for more help in that area.

TOILETING

Toileting and first time potty training can be quite a challenge. There are multiple stimuli involved. Most children with sensory challenges tend to potty train a bit later than average. In addition to the many "typical" recommendations regarding toilet training, you may want to consider these ideas.

- Consider the height of the toilet. A small stool on which to place the feet is more grounding and comforting than dangling feet. Small potty seats that rest on the floor are good for young children, but you will eventually have to make another transition to the regular toilet.

- The wide open space of the bowl itself can be too overwhelming. Place a small inside ring (commercially available) onto the seat, or use a small potty chair when training young children.

- The feel of the unfamiliar plastic on your child's legs and bottom may also be too novel for children first learning. Place one or two opened diapers on the seat as a "covering" but allowing your child to actually urinate into the bowl.

- The sounds in the bathroom may be too overwhelming. Place toilet paper inside toilet before your child sits to dampen sounds. Dampen sounds in the room with towels and carpets. Turn off any noisy air vents. Prepare for the sound of flushing with a song or counting. Allow child to flush the toilet so that there is more control and predictability.

- Placing toilet paper inside the bowl will also prevent any unpleasant tactile sensations by avoiding any splashing up from inside the bowl.

- The smells may also be overwhelming. Keep doors or a window open when possible. Use a preferred fragrance in room if tolerated.

FUNCTIONAL STRATEGIES FOR SCHOOL RELATED TASKS

HOMEWORK HELPERS

Many children have difficulty doing homework for different reasons. These suggestions will focus on the child with sensory modulation dysfunction, but may also be helpful for other children.

Getting Started: This is sometimes the most difficult part. Consider the following suggestions, and modify them as appropriate to your child.

First, consider the timing of homework initiation based on your family's routines and needs. Some parents cannot help with homework until after dinner, some are anxious to get it started and done quickly. How does this match your child's needs? How much help does your child need with homework? All of these factors must be taken into account.

Know your child. How does she typically get off the bus or arrive home? Is she cranky and tired? Wired? Active or sedentary? Many children with sensory modulation dysfunction need some sensory activity before they can transition to homework. Consider that your child needs to move from the "arrival home" state to a "quiet alert" state for homework. How can this happen?

Some pre-homework activities to "wake up" your child might be to provide 10 minutes of lively music. A short marching parade, jumping on a small exercise trampoline, dancing, or jumping jacks might be just right to get her ready to work. Many children do well with a "heavy work" activity or can get better organized if they have a ride on the swings, bicycle, scooter, or roller skates. A spicy snack is alerting, and a chewy snack will help increase readiness and organization to task. Your energetic and enthusiastic tone of voice will also increase your child's readiness to work.

The child who needs some calming time may also do well with an outside activity that uses strong and heavy movements. A proprioceptive and movement activity that is structured and organized will work best. Slow swinging in a hammock or a rocking chair is also very calming. Sucking on a hard candy or lollipop, sipping a drink from a sports sipper bottle, or eating a "chewy" snack such as bagels, fruit leathers, or gum might also help to calm and organize. Relaxing music for 10 to 20 minutes while engaging in a pleasant activity can go a long way towards calming.

Keep It Going: So now that you've started the homework, how do you keep the momentum going? Watch your child's state of alertness. You may need to offer periodic movement or oral strategy breaks when you see your child start to loose organization or attention. You may need to offer a weighted vest during homework. Some children do well with a 5 pound plastic bag of rice placed on their lap to help provide some deep pressure and proprioceptive input to organize them. You can place the bag of rice into a pillow case, large sock, or leg warmer, or sew a small pouch so that it is not too crinkly and slippery.

The environment plays a great role in an individual's ability to stay with a given task. Try to limit distractions where reasonable. These may take the form of visual distractions such as clutter, bright colors, pictures, or even the wrong lighting. Auditory distractions may be background noises, or conversations, humming of fans or fluorescent lights, or the sound of the dishwasher in the background. Be aware of the subtle distractions that may typically go unnoticed by all but your sensory defensive child. That child may be distracted by the itchy clothing, bumpy seat, or feel of the pencil on the paper.

Routines and consistency are always helpful as long as they are not rigid. If your child has a routine time to start homework and a routine place to do it, they are often better able to start the task and focus on it for longer periods of time.

Organization tools are always helpful for all children. You can find the section on organizational strategies within this book. Organization helps a child feel more in control, helps to prevent the stress of those forgotten assignments, books, and papers, and makes everyone involved a lot more comfortable and happy.

Many children with sensory integration dysfunction have great difficulty with handwriting. They may experience fatigue, demonstrate poor legibility, and have immature and inefficient grasps. Try to break the writing tasks up into smaller more manageable segments with breaks between them. For example, if your child has to write ten sentences, do five at a time with a reading task between them. Some teachers allow your child to alternate between writing a sentence and dictating a sentence to the parent. Many teachers modify written tasks with the help of your child's OT and if the IEP allows it. You may want to offer your child some "wake up" activities for the hands between tasks. These exercises/activities can be found in that section of this book.

Use creative strategies to make the homework fun. Sing the spelling words; use rhythms and rhymes to help memorize; use movement to learn the concepts; and engage in complementary activities to reinforce the topics your child is learning. Complementary activities include such things as a visit to the places your child may be studying or cooking a food related to the materials. Many children like contests and games to learn materials. You can model your games after some of the popular game shows on television. For example, you can learn vocabulary words using the old Password game show and learn history facts modeling after "Who Wants to Be a Millionaire?"

Model the behaviors you want to see in your child. Be persistent and attentive. Speak aloud about what you are feeling or doing to keep yourself focused on the task. For example, you may state that you need to stretch your arms or stand up for a minute to help you stay focused. As you become more aware of the strategies you use to maintain your sensory modulation, you will become better able to help your child.

Finish with a Flair: Always acknowledge a job well done. Ultimately you want your child to feel rewarded for a job well done with simple self-satisfaction. Throughout the process, you may need to give a verbal acknowledgement as to the success of the endeavor. Some parents choose to give tangible rewards, such as stickers, prizes, or privileges. This is a parenting choice, but always strive for the internal satisfaction versus the external reward.

ORGANIZATIONAL STRATEGIES

1. **Color Coding-** This is one of the most helpful strategies for organization. Each piece of equipment associated with a subject should all be the same color. For example, the book cover, folder, computer disc, and notebook should all be green for Science, black for Math, and blue for English. Keep this system year to year so that it becomes totally natural for the student. After awhile it just "feels" wrong to place a Science paper in a blue folder. Also color code the daily schedule and keep a copy of it posted in the locker.

2. **Minimize Pieces of Equipment-** Try to minimize the amount of items a student has to remember to bring from place to place. A binder that holds several folders helps. Minimize the amount of pens/pencils and other paraphernalia carried. Make sure the ones that are carried are working well- pens have ink and pencils have points and erasers.

3. **Calendar-** Start a calendar habit as young as possible. Encourage writing all due dates or important dates to remember on a monthly calendar so the entire plan is seen at a glance. Some students need to plan long term projects out on the calendar so that they know how much of each project they should do each night or week. Include extracurricular and family plans so they can see what else will take time in the weeks or months.

4. **Organizers-** Electronic organizers are very helpful and motivating. It minimizes handwriting and keeps all assignments in one basic place. Paper agenda books can be purchased and many schools provide them to encourage

organization. Decide if paper or electronic organizers are best for the student. Paper organizers provide a more spatial and chronological view of the time period, but require more handwriting and tend to fall apart more easily. Electronic organizers require more technological knowledge and require more linear thinking. Electronic organizers can be much more expensive to replace if lost or broken.

5. **Checklists**- Keep a checklist on the student's desk or in a prominent place on his /her binder with a checklist for going home. Some students keep one taped in their locker. This should list *briefly*, in a word or two, the items for bringing home. It can be color coded.

6. **Routines**-Develop consistent routines. When routines are in place, the student will become more automatic and faster in completing those rote daily activities. One routine should be to check supplies each night after homework for the next day. Place the backpack and next day materials in the same place each night for the next morning. Putting clothing out for the next day the night before often improves a very hectic morning. Try to keep to a schedule for each day.

7. **Paperwork**- Organizing paper work or the placement of written work on a paper requires much organization. Many students do well placing math problems on graph paper or using loose-leaf paper sideways to keep columns. There are many different lined papers and notebooks that help organize the spacing in handwriting.

8. **To Do Lists:** Make a daily checklist of things to do. Make each task small and manageable so as to gain success. For example, instead of listing "clean room," break the task

down into several smaller steps. The list might read: make bed, pick up items from floor, put away laundry, put away books, put away toys. You can place a big heading over each sublist of tasks to get the big picture. Everyone feels rewarded when they can finish the list and cross off completed tasks. Be careful not to make the list unreasonably extensive.

9. **Minimize Clutter:** Clutter is frequently a major contributor to disorganization. Set frequent scheduled times to clean out backpacks, desks, lockers, etc. Have a separate folder for take home, keep home, and back to school. Provide bins or shelving at home to keep similar belongings together. Throw out items no longer needed.

10. **Modeling and Encouragement:** Parents and teachers do a great deal for students by modeling organized strategies. Adults should use these same concepts as a model. Provide encouragement for the student to develop their own ideas that work for them. Sometimes students need trial and error to learn the best methods for themselves. Develop problem solving for any task that needs an organized approach.

Some websites:

www.organizedteens.com
www.unclutter.com
www.getorganizednow.com

Sensory Integration Activities

There are many enjoyable activities that are easy to do and offer your child opportunities for enhanced sensory intake. They should be incorporated into your child's day in a fun and playful way. Daily "doses" of tactile, vestibular, and proprioceptive activities can go a long way towards helping your child overcome the challenges of DSI. The following are some suggestions you might like to enjoy with your child that also will help develop sensory integration.

PROPRIOCEPTIVE ACTIVITIES

Proprioceptive sensory intake gives information about the movement, location, and forces exerted on the joints and muscles. It has a calming and organizing influence on the nervous system, and helps to develop the sense of where the body is. It also helps develop motor planning.

"Heavy work" activities are those that make the muscles and joints work hard against resistance. They provide significant proprioceptive input. Some ideas for these activities are:

*carrying heavy or weighted objects such as a pile of books , groceries, backpack, or playing with weighted balls or toys

*pushing hard against resistance such as pushing a heavy wagon or cart, moving furniture, pushing against the wall or desk, chair push-ups, pumping swings

*pulling heavy objects such as a wagon or sled uphill or pulling in Tug-O-War

*climbing or hanging on monkey bars, stretching

*working with clay, squeezing water toys or stress balls, kneading bread, stirring stiff food products such as crisped rice cereal snacks

*jumping on a trampoline, or off of a step, hopping, hopscotch

*raking leaves, shoveling snow, vacuuming, sweeping, mopping

*digging in bins of rice or beans, finding objects "buried" in rice bins, digging in the garden or in the sand

*erasing the chalkboard or washing desks or table tops

*heavy marching, running hard

*push-ups, sit-ups, chin-ups, dips, jumping jacks, wheel-barrow walks

*games such as tug of war, leap frog, play wrestling

*biking, roller skating, ice skating

*wearing weighted wearables while moving

*yoga, some forms of Karate

For Teens: Working with weights after age 14
              The Pilates workouts

VESTIBULAR ACTIVITIES

These are movement activities. The vestibular system has a powerful influence on alertness, visual skills, attention, bilateral coordination, and balance.

*active movement is integrated better than passive, imposed movement

*sports activities such as roller skating, swimming, bicycle riding, gymnastics, scooters, dancing, etc. all combine vestibular with proprioceptive input

*rolling on the floor or down a hill, rolling UP the hill adds more proprioception

* hopping, jumping, skipping, jumping jacks, tumblesaults

*rocking in rocking chair or hammock

*playground equipment such as slides, swings, seesaw, etc.

*balance activities such as walking a curb or balance beam, standing on one foot

*bouncing on bed, small exercise trampoline, or therapy ball

*hopscotch, jump rope, hippity hop

*play rough housing with strict rules to prevent over stimulation or fear

TACTILE ACTIVITIES

The tactile system works with the proprioceptive system to develop motor planning. It involves the sense of touch, and it helps individuals feel comfortable in the environment. Deep pressure touch is very calming and organizing.

*wearing a weighted vest or placing a weighted bean bag on the lap while concentrating on homework or table activity, weighted blankets

*hug vests made from neoprene give deep pressure touch

*"sandwich squash" is an activity where the child is "squashed" (deep pressure) between two pieces of "bread" (large pillows, cushions, or bean bag chairs)

*fiddling with textured objects such as the popular Stress Balls (or a deflated balloon filled with flour, small beans, or rice). Do not use for children who mouth objects or are under 3 years old.

*firm rubs with towel after bath, firm lotion rubs

*bear hugs, self hugs

*wrap up in towels or blankets

*roll up in blanket to make a hot dog; press firmly on child's back to put on imaginary mustard and ketchup, etc.

*resistive activities (see Proprioceptive activities section) *firm massages

*crawling into a stretchy fabric "bag" (make a great bag out of spandex fabric). You can also use a t-shirt fabric pillow case

*play with assorted texture toys or materials to tolerance; provide deep pressure first.

*wear spandex shirts or shorts under clothing

AUDITORY ACTIVITIES

*use music to calm or alert as needed, combine with vestibular/proprioceptive/tactile activities; there are many commercially available music products to try

*use music to help transition ex. Mickey Mouse goodbye song, clean up song, Good   Night Ladies song

*hum to soothe hurts or help tolerate unpleasant necessities (hair washing, etc.)

*sing about everyday routines; You can use the old nursery rhyme "Here We Go Round the Mulberry Bush" and sing "this is the way we wash our hair, go to school, etc.)

*tap rhythms for spelling or times tables (memorizing)

*sing the steps to learning, such as in "ABC" song

*have a special song for special tasks- make it up to another tune you know

*use musical instruments to develop motor skills and rhythm

*listening programs such as Berard, Tomatis, The Listening Program, Samonas, or Therapeutic Listening. More information on these is available in the Auditory section

*Don Campbell's Mozart Effect programs

*Advanced Brain Technologies Sound Health Series or Music for Babies

VISUAL ACTIVITIES

*combine visual with vestibular activities

*use a flashlight in a dark room for visual focus and tracking. Spot things on the wall or floor to label. Put the light spot in child's reach. When child steps on the spot or touches it, quickly turn off light and say "you got it!"

*puzzles, mazes, dot to dots, find the hidden picture are all good visual perceptual activities

*play "I see something…" game

*games such as Light Bright

*lava lamps or commercially available novelty lamps

*toys that light up or glow in the dark

SENSORY ORAL MOTOR ACTIVITIES

The following suggestions are designed to provide an oral motor program that offers a variety of sensory experiences. Each activity has a specific sensory goal.

1. CHEWING

Chewing has an organizing effect on the nervous system. It also provides for proprioceptive and tactile intake. Offer chewing activities when a child seeks proprioception or when disorganized.

a) gum
b) chewy candies
c) dried fruit
d) granola bars
e) bagels

2. BLOWING also provides proprioception and develop breath support.

a) bubbles with assorted wands
b) assorted whistles, kazoos, flutes, etc.
c) blow toy party favors; play a game blowing Styrofoam packing pellets, cotton balls, or feathers with party favor off the table.
d) blow through straws in the same manner. Another idea for straws is to place water color paint on a cardboard in small "puddles." Blow through the straw to move the paint into beautiful patterns. Also, blow bubbles in a cup of liquid (edible, in case they suck some up). Blow through a straw to move ping pong balls placed on the table or floating in a

basin of water.

3. SUCKING has a calming influence and provide for proprioceptive and tactile stimulation.

a) hard candy (if appropriate and safe)
b) frozen ice pops
c) peanut or other nut butters to suck and lick off the fingers, check for allergies.
d) sucking thick liquids through a straw adds additional intensity and is highly recommended; thick shakes, applesauce, baby food purees, yogurt, pudding are all good.
e) use a sport sipper bottle as often as possible
f) suck through a straw to create enough suction to pick up scraps of paper or a ping pong ball and drop it into a bowl by releasing that suction
g) crazy straws of unusual and assorted shapes or designs

4. CRUNCHING is an alerting activity. Use this when the child needs a "boost" to help develop an appropriate level of attention and arousal.

a) popcorn
b) crackers
c) pretzels
d) nuts
e) raw vegetables
f) ice cubes

5. LICKING is a sophisticated oral motor skill used to explore and alert.

a) lollipops

b) licking pudding, syrup, honey, or other thick liquids off the fingers
c) ice pops

6. TASTE has different influences on individuals. General guidelines are:

a) sour, bitter, and spicy foods tend to be alerting
b) sweet foods increase drooling and are sometimes calming
c) it is wise to observe how different, textures, spices and flavors influence a child, and adjust the diet accordingly

7. VIBRATION increases sensory awareness, and can be alerting or calming depending on the rhythm and frequency.

a) electric toothbrush
b) massaging/vibrating teething toys
c) fizzing candies

SENSORY VESTS

Many parents ask about the use of weighted vests and sensory vests that have become quite popular. It is important to understand the rationale for the use and the mechanics of how to use the vests properly.

The **weighted vest** is a tool frequently used in sensory integration programs. It is designed to provide deep pressure tactile and proprioceptive input for a child who needs it. The weighted vest is intended to provide a calming and organizing influence on the individual. It also helps to provide additional sensory information to develop an increased sense of body awareness. A weighted vest should only be used under the guidance of your treating therapist.

The vest should be fitted securely over the shoulders and across the torso. It should not hang off the shoulders or slide around on the body. It should not rest on the seat when sitting in a chair. The weights in the vest must be distributed evenly in all pockets. The same weight should be in each pocket. The amount of weight tolerated should be assessed by the Occupational Therapist. The general rule of thumb for weight is no more than 5% of the child's bodyweight. A good starting place is one pound for preschoolers and 3 pounds for teens.

The vest can be worn for approximately 20-30 minutes at a time. It should then be removed for approximately 1-1/2 to 2 hours and can be worn again for another 20-30 minutes. Consult your therapist for specific wearing time, as it can vary for each child. This can be done throughout the day. Some people prefer to use the vest

Sensory Integration Strategies for Parents

when engaged in selected activities that require concentration and attention. The calming influence helps maintain attention to task.

Do not wear the vest when engaged in excessive gross motor activity, near a pool or body of water, or when sleeping. Do not use the vest on any person with a cardiac problem, severe scoliosis, or severe joint deformities. Children with low muscle tone or alignment problems should only wear the vest as prescribed by the treating therapist. Although unlikely, consult the prescribing therapist if donning the vest or wearing the vest causes agitation or stress.

The **Pressure vest or Hug vest** is also used in sensory integration programs. It does not have weight, but instead, provides deep tactile pressure through its material makeup. It can be worn under or over clothing and can be worn for longer periods of time. This is because the input it gives is more variable.

The decision to use a vest, which one to use, and how to use it is usually determined by the treating therapist.

"WAKE UP" ACTIVITIES for THE HANDS

These suggestions will provide increased sensory awareness to the hands and fingers before beginning fine motor activities such as handwriting. They do not all have to be don; but choose those that are most effective.

- Manipulate therapy putty or clay. Squeezing against resistance is "heavy work" for the hands. Commonly available "stress balls" or squeezing toys will also work.

- Shake out hands and fingers in quick rapid shakes. Open and close fists rapidly.

- Rub lotion firmly into hands and fingers. Rub each finger individually.

- Stretch out rubber bands or Theraband tubing with fingers. Be careful of the rubber bands flying where you do not want them.

- Press fingertips together. Spread fingers apart and together while maintaining pressure on each tip. Flex and extend fingers as in the itsy bitsy spider while maintaining the same pressure.

- Provide quick joint compressions and tractions to each finger. Joint compressions are done by pushing into the finger joints from the tip of the finger into the hand. The finger must be held straight. Follow with gentle traction. This is pulling gently on the fingers, away from the hand.

■ Pop plastic packaging material bubbles.

SPECIAL CONSIDERATIONS REGARDING THE AUDITORY SYSTEM

There are many questions regarding auditory processing, auditory defensive behavior, and auditory interventions. This is to clarify some of these questions.

CENTRAL AUDITORY PROCESSING

What is auditory processing?

Auditory processing is the term used to describe how your brain recognizes and interprets the sounds around you. We need to "process" auditory information, or sounds, in order to understand language, have a conversation, be alert for dangers in the environment, and feel comfortable in our environment.

What is Central Auditory Processing Disorder (CAPD)?

CAPD is a problem with the interpretation of sounds. Hearing acuity is fine, but the understanding of auditory information is inefficient. It is a problem in *processing*.

What are some signs of CAPD?

These are some signs. A child may have only some of them. One sign alone cannot indicate CAPD - we need to see several.

- Asks "what" frequently
- Inconsistent responses to auditory stimuli
- Often misunderstands what is said
- Requests information be repeated
- Poor listening and auditory attention
- Distractibility
- Difficulty following oral instructions
- Difficulty listening in background noise
- Difficulty in phonics and speech sound discrimination
- Poor auditory memory

- Poor sequencing
- Poor expressive and receptive language skills
- Slow or delayed response to verbal requests
- Reading, spelling, or other academic problems
- Learns poorly through auditory channel
- Behavioral problems can occur secondarily

What strategies can I use to help my child who has auditory processing dysfunction?

- Seat child away from distracting sounds in the classroom or when listening to a speaker
- Seat child near the teacher in the classroom
- Get the child's full attention (eye contact or touch helps) before speaking
- Simplify instructions, using one step directions if necessary
- Have the student repeat what is necessary to be heard
- Use visual or manipulative aids to reinforce auditory information
- Give breaks from intense listening throughout the day
- Speak distinctly and simply – do not over exaggerate speech
- Use key words and outlines for note taking; some students like to have a note taking buddy
- Use consistent routines and structure
- Reduce background noise when possible
- Provide processing time
- Teach listening skills (i.e. waiting for speaker to stop, using body language, looking at mouth and eyes)
- Minimize the need to have the child write and listen at the same time

- Encourage asking questions
- Vary loudness to increase attention
- Use clear gestures to emphasize verbal information
- "Pre-teach" educational lessons or provide written work and/or vocabulary to review before teaching via auditory means

What treatments are available?

- Auditory interventions training programs (see Auditory Interventions section)

- Earobics (Cognitive Concepts) www.earobics.com

- Fast ForWord (Scientific Learning) www.scilearn.com

- Lindamood-Bell Method www.lindamoodbell.com

- Auditory or FM trainer systems

- Speech and language therapy

AUDITORY DEFENSIVENESS

What is auditory defensiveness or auditory defensive behavior?

Auditory defensiveness is a sensory integration problem where an individual is overly sensitive to sounds. The nervous system of a child with auditory defensive behavior interprets sounds, that most people would typically tolerate, to be noxious.

What are some signs of auditory defensiveness?

A child might have some of these reactions. One sign alone would not indicate the problem, but several of them could be related to auditory defensive behavior.

- Bothered by sounds of fluorescent lights, fans, or blowers/heaters, beepers. etc
- Distracted by sounds not typically noticed by others
- Poor attention, poor listening
- Agitated by sounds in cafeteria, gym class, swimming pools, public restrooms, school bus etc.
- Bothered by auditory reverberation
- Difficulty following verbal directions
- May sometimes tune out sounds and not respond
- Talks excessively or make excessive noises
- Difficulty in phonics and academic subjects

What can I do to help my child?

- Enlist the help of teachers and aides to understand the problem

- Be supportive and encouraging
- Minimize time spent in noisy environments
- Use carpets and fabric to absorb sound in noisy environments (i.e. towels and carpets in bathrooms)
- Use headphones with acceptable music on bus
- Cut tennis balls to place on legs of chairs in classroom
- Seat child away from noises in classroom (fans, windows, fidgety children)
- Seat child near the door in cafeteria
- Chew gum or chewy foods when in noisy environment
- Speak softly and clearly

What treatment is available?

- Home or school based auditory intervention or listening programs such as The Listening Program, SAMONAS method, or Therapeutic Listening
- Clinic based auditory intervention training such as Dynamic Listening Systems, Berard and Tomatis methods
- Occupational therapy using sensory integration techniques

THERAPEUTIC AUDITORY INTERVENTIONS

Music has been used therapeutically for many years. Since the 1960's however, specially treated music has become available. Dr. Alfred Tomatis was the originator of this concept and most, if not all, listening or auditory interventions available today are based on his work. These auditory interventions provide sounds and music that are chosen for specific, special qualities and treated in different ways to help individuals process auditory information better. The methods vary as do the schedules and equipment for listening. Children with sensory processing dysfunction often do well with these programs. The auditory apparatus and the vestibular apparatus are located together in the ear and they run neurologically together throughout the brain. These two systems interact and influence each other. The auditory interventions are often seen to help individuals with vestibular and other sensory issues in addition to the auditory concerns.

The following is an overview of some of the most well known and researched interventions used today. All of these methods described require that an authorized or certified practitioner administer and/or supervise the program. These practitioners are trained in the methods they provide.

TOMATIS METHOD: Alfred Tomatis, a French ENT doctor, began his work in the 1950's and 60's. It is upon his work that most interventions are designed today. He used specially treated music to "re-educate the ear." Tomatis recognized the close relationship between the listening/hearing portion of the ear (cochlear system) and the movement/balance portion of the ear (vestibular system). He connected listening to the development of language, learning, motor control, and attention. He also recognized that the brain needs sound energy to help the thinking process. His listening device is called the electronic ear. The Tomatis approach is administered in a clinic over a period of time on a daily basis. He uses the mother's voice, classical music, and bone conduction of sound, as well as the filtered music through headphones.

BERARD METHOD (AUDITORY INTEGRATION or AIT): Dr. Guy Berard felt that the Tomatis protocol was not efficient enough so he developed a different system of filtering the music. He developed the Audiokinetron and the Earducator, which can use popular music. He believed that hypersensitive hearing can cause auditory processing problems. This method is also a clinic based treatment, usually provided for 10 consecutive days, twice a day, 30 minutes at each session. Annebel Stehli's book, "The Sound of a Miracle," was about the benefits her daughter received from AIT. Her book helped to bring public attention to this approach.

THERAPEUTIC LISTENING: Sheila Frick, OTR (occupational therapist) developed this program based on Dr. Tomatis' teachings, her Berard training, and in consultation with Ingo Steinbach (a German sound engineer). It uses a number of electronically altered CDs in a specific trained manner, that is tailored to the individual. They are suitable for use at home or in school. It is suggested that this program be used in conjunction with sensory integration treatment. An initial program may be in place for 2 to 6 months, but many may continue longer. Listening is typically accomplished through high quality headphones for

20-30 minutes, twice a day. The beauty of this program is that it can be administered at home by parents, under the preparation and supervision of a trained practitioner. The music ranges from children's songs, to classical music, to nature sounds, to electronic music. Therapeutic Listening also offers some CDs designed to help with sensory modulation that can be used without headphones.

SAMONAS: This approach, developed by Ingo Steinbach, has combined the ideas of Dr. Tomatis with more recent advances in technology and physics. Steinbach was very particular regarding the musicians used, the places where recordings took place, and the intent of the musicians. He developed the envelope shape modulator, which enhances the upper frequency ranges. He calls this spectrally activated. He created several levels of CDs, which can be used at home. A SAMONAS practioner can provide this program. This program can also be used at home with headphones and CD player.

THE LISTENING PROGRAM (TLP): This program was developed by Advanced Brain Technologies (ABT). Unlike many others, it was developed by a team of professionals in fields such as neurology, psychiatry, neurodevelopment, education, speech pathology, psychoacoustics, music, and sound engineering. It is also built on the work of Dr. Tomatis. TLP uses state of the art technology to enhance classical music as well as nature sounds. TLP offers home based programs that can be listened to once or twice a day, for 15 minute sessions, for 5 out of 7 days a week. The program takes a minimum of 8 to 16 weeks. The program can be repeated as needed and timing is individually determined. There are additional CDs, specifically designed to be used to increase sensory integration and language. ABT also offers Music for Babies and The Sound Health Series, which can be used without headphones. Advanced Brain Technologies also offers a clinic-based intervention called Dynamic Listening System.

Auditory Intervention Websites

TOMATIS
www.spectrumcenter.com
www.auditoryprocessing.org

BERARD
www.sait.org
www.ideatrainingcenter.com
www.guyberard.com

THE LISTENING PROGRAM AND DYNAMIC LISTENING SYSTEM
www.advancedbrain.com

THERAPEUTIC LISTENING
www.vitallinks.org

A BAKER'S DOZEN

Concepts of Sensory Integration for Parents

1. KNOWLEDGE. Know your child. Learn what your child reacts to and how. Trust yourself.

2. RESPECT. Respect your child. If a child feels that something is scary or hurtful, honor that feeling and do not belittle it. It is real to them. Try to comment, "I know this is scary for you but let's see how we can make you feel more comfortable," or "let's see if we can try it together!"

3. ATTITUDE. Be *positive* and *calm*. While you understand your child's needs, you also have to let them know that they can do it! They can read you and pick up on your emotions. Communicate strength and empowerment! They can also feel your stress. Get support for yourself and find ways to help you deal with your stress or anxieties.

4. EDUCATE. Educate your child and those around him. Help your child to understand his sensory needs, at his developmental level, and in a positive way. Help her learn to self-advocate. Educate those around your child as needed, especially those in authority over your child.

5. PREPARE. Prepare your child for events or activities ahead of time. Predictability and routines help alleviate sensory defensiveness. Be very careful not to overdue this, however, as strict routines and excessive need for sameness or predictability can be just as damaging as dealing with the sensory challenges.

6. ANALYZE. Problem solve. Analyze reactions, try strategies, consult with others such as your child's therapist. Each child is unique.

7. ADJUST. Minimize time spent in stressful situations. Use "grading" or little by little increases in time to increase tolerance. You may have to be strong when you tell family and friends that it is time to leave, or that you cannot do some things right now.

8. ADAPT. Develop strategies specific to your child. Every child is unique. The strategies provided here are only guidelines. You must develop your child's own individual plan.

9. MODIFY. Modify the environment as possible and reasonable. Use "grading" here as well. Little by little decrease those modifications. The goal is to have your child function in society with as few modifications as possible.

10. CREATE. Be adaptive. Challenge your thoughts about "how it is *supposed* to be done." Think outside the box.

11. TEACH. Teach to your child's strengths. An auditory defensive child may learn better through the visual or tactile channel. A tactile defensive child may learn better through listening or looking.

12. MODEL. Model strategies. Verbalize how you use sensory strategies that work for you – and use them. For example, you may say, " I don't like so much noise in here. I think I will turn off the TV." Or you may say, "I feel too excited right now; I think I will take some deep breaths to

calm myself down."

13. OPEN YOUR MIND. Remember that children are multifaceted, and while sensory integration difficulties are present, your child may also benefit from additional approaches, strategies, and ideas.

CONCLUSION

Sensory integration dysfunction and its treatment will most likely take you and your child down many roads on a journey of self-discovery for your child, yourself, and your family. Sensory integration dysfunction and its treatment is very unique to each individual and to each family. There is no one treatment that is the perfect approach, and there are many strategies that can be used to help your child meet with maximal success and satisfaction in life. I hope that this book provides you with some ideas and resources for your journey. I am sure that you will discover many strategies and ideas as you travel. I am always happy to hear of your successes and ideas. You may write to me at Occupational Therapy Strategies, PC, PO Box 12414, Hauppauge, NY 11788.

Sensory Integration Strategies for Parents

GLOSSARY OF TERMS

This glossary was prepared to further explain terms as used in this publication.

Auditory: the sense of hearing; having to do with hearing of sounds

Bilateral Integration: the skill of coordinating both sides of the body

Dyspraxia: a sensory integration disorder that stems from problems in the processing of primarily the tactile and proprioceptive systems. It causes poor motor planning.

Joint Stability: the ability to stabilize or hold a joint in place by the action of muscles, ligaments, and tendons working together around the joint

Midline Crossing: the ability to reach across the middle of the body with arms and hands. May also be used to reflect the ability to use the eyes to read or scan across the middle of a page or line

Muscle Tone: the readiness of muscles to move and act; the natural state of muscles that may vary from high to low in different individuals

Olfactory: having to do with the sense of smell

Oral Praxis: the ability to motor plan movements of the mouth, lips, and tongue

Praxis: also known as motor planning; the ability to figure out how to use the body and hands in novel motor tasks that are skilled actions

Proprioception: a sensory system that interprets movement of the limbs and body; helps in the planning of motor actions

Sensorimotor Integration Activities: activities that keep in mind the role of the sensory systems as well as the individual's sensory needs

Sensory Integration: a theory of normal development; an evaluation and treatment approach for people who have deficits in this process, which involves very specifically selected activities designed to help the nervous system learn to process sensory information efficiently for adaptive use

Sensory Modulation: the ability of the brain to govern, coordinate, and monitor it's own reactions

Tactile: pertaining to the sense of touch; involves a protective and a discriminatory function

Vestibular: sensory system that detects movement and position of the head

Visual: having to do with the eye or seeing; the sense of sight

About the Author

Jeanne Sangirardi Ganz, OTR/L, BCP has been a pediatric Occupational Therapist working with children with sensory processing dysfunction for over 25 years and is board certified in pediatrics. She is also certified in sensory integration testing and neurodevelopmental treatment (NDT). Jeanne has studied auditory interventions and is a certified provider for The Listening Program. She is the author of the book, "Including SI: A guide to Using Sensory Integration Strategies in School," written for therapists. Ms. Ganz has lectured extensively to parents and professionals and maintains a private practice.

Disclaimer

The ideas presented in this book are based on sensory processing and behavioral concepts. The reader is cautioned that not all suggestions are appropriate to all individuals and consult with a professional is recommended. Neither the author, nor the publisher, imply any direct or indirect endorsement of a specific recommendation or activity for an individual person.